Contents

Dedication

For Duane Douglas Carpenter

His life was gentle, and the elements
So mixed in him, that Nature might stand up,
And say to all the world: This was a man.

William Shakespeare, *Julius Caesar*, Act 5

Introduction
The Book's Approach

If you are a teacher, coach, or administrator of a sport program, or a student preparing for one of these professions, this book is written for you. Material that would be of use only to attorneys is omitted, as is material that would be of use only to those concerned with professional athletes. You should spend your time and energy efficiently, so the topics have been selected carefully, and the depth and breadth of discussions are based on what is useful to you as a teacher, coach, and administrator.

The title, *Legal Concepts in Sport: A Primer,* was not chosen lightly. Rather, the title represents the strong belief that an effective book on law and sport must deal with concepts. Once you understand a legal concept, you can apply it to evaluate a situation in your school or program. If you only received rules gleaned from past cases ("don't put a chair under the basketball backboard or you might be sued for negligence" or "always put a contract in writing"), you wouldn't gain an understanding of the law. Without a conceptual understanding of the law, you would be less able to evaluate the legal implications involved in the differing sets of circumstances you face in your school.

This book is committed to the conceptual approach. When a case is presented, it is not provided as a rule but as an illustration or a scenario with which to practice your newly acquired conceptual understanding.

The importance of the conceptual approach goes beyond its ease of application to your situation. The "rules" (precedents) found in court cases apply within the jurisdiction of the court but not beyond; thus, a rule in Oregon may not be the rule in Pennsylvania. But a conceptual view of the law is more universal and will apply wherever you are. And although the book is written in a light style, the author takes seriously her task of helping you learn and retain important legal concepts that you need to know.

The Book's Scope

When most people think of legal issues in sport they think about negligence. However, in your professional life, you will face a much broader range of issues. For instance, topics such as sexual harassment, corporal punishment, and products liability are of special importance today. Anti-discrimination laws and the concepts involved in contracting to buy equipment or deciding to fire a coach are important for today's teacher, coach, and administrator. You'll find these legal concepts and many others developed on the pages of this book.

How to Use the Book

The first two chapters deal broadly with concepts of our legal system. Chapters 3 through 13 discuss specific concepts in detail, and the final chapter deals with managing the risks of potential imposition of legal fault and unwanted legal obligation.

Practice scenarios, memory ticklers, reviews, and memory testers with discussions are liberally added throughout the chapters to help you understand the concepts more easily. The practice scenarios present an opportunity for you to test your understanding of a principle. The memory ticklers are short outlines of the elements or main points of certain concepts.

Reviews appear after explanation and discussion of a specific concept and summarize the significant facts and theories; some reviews are in the middle of a chapter (interim reviews) and some are at the end. The memory testers are provided in a form that allows you to check whether or not you understand the major points presented. These sections include mostly true/false questions, but may also contain a few short answer questions. Following the questions, you will find a brief discussion of the true/false answers, but no discussion of the short answer questions. You will need to refer to the text to confirm your understanding of these short answer questions.

At the end of most chapters, there is also a list of legal cases to which you may wish to refer for additional insights. Some of these cases are classics because of their value as precedents or because of their clear and complete explanation of a particular legal issue. Others are current, cutting edge cases which have value because they provide insight into the changing nature of the law. The cases cited are available in print through law and academic libraries, as well as through internet sites which require no special access provisions. So whether or not you are lucky enough to have access to a law library or specialized proprietary electronic libraries, you will have access to the cases used.

About the Author

Lawyers have written in the area of sports *law*. Physical educators have written in the area of *sports* law. Linda Jean Carpenter brings a universality to her treatment of sports law because she has both a PhD degree in physical education and a JD degree. Carpenter is a professor emerita from the Department of Physical Education and Exercise Science, Brooklyn College of the City University of New York, and an attorney and member of the New York State Bar and the U.S. Supreme Court Bar.

The author's expertise and experience in both sport and the law give her a unique combination for writing this book. Her ability to focus on the truly important legal issues in sport arises from her roots in physical education. Her ability to discuss those issues in a legally accurate, up-to-date context arises from her full legal background. Her ability to put knowledge and experience into a concise and useful framework with which you can evaluate the legal issues in your own situations arises from her perspective as a teacher and coach.

Chapter 1

Our Legal System: The Basics

The purpose of this book is to give the reader a conceptual foundation for understanding the law and its relationship to sport and physical education programs. The book will attempt to place the kinds of legal problems faced in the day-to-day operations of a physical education or athletic program into a commonsense perspective that is easily understood and remembered. It is not intended to teach all there is to know about the law, but instead to serve as an introduction to the areas of law that most often have an impact on administrators, teachers, and coaches.

What Is Law?

Relationships

The law is many different things. It may be thought of as a system for defining relationships between people. For example, if a person is hurt because another person has been careless, the injured person may assert a right to be compensated for injuries. If the

1

injured person takes the case to court, the court will decide whether or not the careless person had a duty to protect the injured person from being hurt. If the court finds that the careless person had no duty to look out for the safety of the injured person, then the injured person's claim for compensation will fail. There may be many reasons why the court would make such a determination, but by not finding such a duty the court/jury is saying that the "relationship" between the parties was not of the type that would require the payment of compensation.

Prohibited Behavior

Another way of answering the question "What is law?" is to regard it as a system of principles that tells us how to behave. For example, the law tells us that we cannot commit crimes. A criminal act is one that is defined by the law as being evil, or that creates such undesirable consequences that it should be prohibited. Our system of criminal laws tells us how to behave and the punishment that we must suffer for misbehaving.

Reasonableness of Behavior

The law also tells us that we must behave in a reasonable manner even when we are not committing crimes. For example, one should not drive a car at the speed limit if the road is covered with ice. It may not be reasonable to drive that fast, and the court would probably say that the driver was legally at fault should an accident occur. Again, the law is telling us how to behave.

Creation and Limitation of Freedom

Yet another way to answer the question "What is law?" is to regard it as a system that both creates and limits freedom. The law, principally through our Constitution, ensures that we will enjoy the basic freedoms of being a citizen of our state and nation. However, our freedoms are not unlimited. For example, the right to free expression does not guarantee to us the right to slander our neighbor. Our rights as citizens are extensive, but they are limited by the law so that

What is Law?

Relationships
Prohibited behavior
Reasonableness of behavior
Creation and limitation of freedom

we may realize the greatest degree of freedom consistent with the freedom of our fellow citizens.

Why Do We Have Laws?

Once we have tentatively answered the question "What is law?" we may ask, "Why do we need laws?" To a certain degree these questions are very similar. The law's reason for being seems to be given when we describe what it is. But there is more to the question of why we have laws than first appears.

Goodness

When a court decides a case, its decision is closely tied to the reason for the existence of laws. For example, the court's decision may be based on issues of good versus evil. Our laws prohibit the killing of one person by another. However, if someone were to attack you using deadly force, then the law allows you to defend yourself, even to the extent of killing your attacker. The evil intent of your attacker is considered when determining whether you are guilty of the crime of murder.

Fairness

In addition to considerations of good and evil, the law may take into account what is fair. The law may be said to be a great equalizer, leveling the playing field so that the wealthiest or strongest does not always prevail. Our federal Constitution guarantees each of us equal protection of the laws. This means that we are each able to assert our rights under the law, without our race, sex, national origin, or other irrelevant factors being weighed against us. Fairness is the main consideration when laws are created to eliminate discrimination in schools or in the workplace.

Consistency

The law also takes into consideration the need for consistency. If the law were not consistent, people would not know what kinds of activities were illegal. Furthermore, it would be almost impossible to conduct business. Laws are generally created to see to it that there is consistent enforcement of an underlying policy. To illustrate the theme of consistency in the law, take the situation in which two people enter into a written contract for the sale of softball uniforms. If the contract fails to state the price of the uniforms, it does not necessarily mean that the contract is unenforceable. The law will require merely that a "reasonable" price should be paid for the uniforms. In this way the law tells people who engage in the sale of goods that even though they may fail to state all the terms of their bargain, their contracts will still create legal obligations if the term they have failed to state may be ascertained. In this situation, a "reasonable price" is ascertainable, and the transaction must be completed. In the overall scheme of things, it is in the best interests of society to enforce contracts that are close to being complete. The laws' uniform adherence to this policy of enforcing contracts brings consistency to the marketplace and allows the engines of commerce to run smoothly.

Enforcement

A similar reason for having laws is the desire to provide a means by which promises can be enforced. In the example previously mentioned, two people entered into a contract for the sale of softball uniforms. A contract is a promise that creates a legal obligation to perform. When two or more parties contract to perform certain duties, for example, to deliver money for uniforms, their promises become enforceable by a court of law. Of course, this is provided all the legal requirements of a contract are met. Contracts will be discussed later, but it is important to remember that certain promises will be enforced by the law, and this is one of the reasons for having laws.

Compensation

Another important reason we have laws relates to the idea that if one person causes injury to another, then the injured person should be compensated. The objective of the law is to "make the injured person whole." For example, if a careless person has caused another person to break a leg, then the careless person should pay the cost of medical expenses, lost wages, and for the pain and suffering that have resulted. This is the basic conceptual theme underlying the law of "torts," which will be discussed later.

Ownership

An important reason for having laws concerns the ownership of property. Property may be things such as books, shoes, cars, or basketballs; property may also be land. Objects such as books are called "personal property," while land is called "real property." Both kinds of property require many different kinds of laws in order for people to enjoy and make use of their property. For example, a person who enters onto the land of another without permission is said to be a "trespasser," and the land owner can file a lawsuit against the intruder. If a person takes your radio and sells it to someone else, the taker has committed "larceny" and may be prosecuted for committing a crime. Because the larcenist has taken your personal property, the taker may also be sued by you for "conversion" and be required to pay you the value of the radio. In a conceptual way, ownership applies also to the more esoteric notion of property right. For instance, if you are a tenured teacher, you have an interest in the "property" of your continued employment. Your ownership of that property interest, ie. your continued employment, is stronger than a similar property interest of a teacher in the middle of a one year contract. Your connection to the property interest of your continued employment as a tenured teacher is greater than the untenured teacher in the middle of a one-year contract, but both of you have some degree of property rights which are in many ways similar to the land owner or the owner of a basketball. Each of these situations involves the use and enjoyment of property. When people interfere with your use and enjoyment of your property, the law provides a means by which you may recover your losses.

Why Do We Have Laws?

Goodness
Fairness
Consistency
Enforcement
Compensation
Ownership

Where Does the Law Come From?

After considering the reasons for having laws, we should now consider the sources of laws. There are, in fact, several sources of laws. When we look to the beginnings of our civilization, we realize that whether our ancestors lived in a time of order or a time of chaos has depended on whether there was regular enforcement of a system of laws. When there was law, there was order. It has been suggested that certain laws existed among our ancestors before the development of courts, or what we consider our modern system of law. This so-called natural law focused on respect for the individual person and for the ownership of "private" property. These laws have been referred to, among other things, as "certain unalienable rights" and include the right to life, liberty, and the pursuit of happiness.

Natural law is therefore the foundation upon which all other law is based. It represents the first step humankind took away from the uncivilized notions that "might makes right." When people first created unity and order in tribal communities, they made the conscious decision that certain individual freedoms would necessarily have to be curtailed for the good of the community.

The interrelationship of individual freedoms and the community's interests became the focus of more sophisticated societies as they developed legal systems. Mesopotamian, Egyptian, Greek, and Roman laws reflected the concern that the rights of citizens should be accorded value and be respected by the state.

Distribution of Power via the Constitution

The evolution of law eventually led to the creation of constitutional documents. A constitution is a statement that causes certain powers possessed by the people to be delegated to the government in order that the people may benefit from an ordered system of liberty. The U.S. Constitution begins with the words, "We the people." By beginning in this manner, it states clearly that the people possess the ultimate power in this nation.

In its Preamble, our Constitution states its intention of ensuring domestic tranquility, providing for the common defense, promoting the general welfare, and securing the blessing of liberty to the people. The Preamble also states that it is the intention of the Constitution to "establish justice."

More than a statement of intentions, the Constitution actually states how the power given to government is to be used. It establishes the Congress, the Presidency, and the Supreme Court. It gives power to Congress to make laws to accomplish certain objectives, and it gives the President authority to command the military and to administer the government by creating regulations. The Supreme

Court is given the power to review the laws made by Congress and the regulations made by the President to determine if they are consistent with the Constitution's original intent. The Court is therefore a very important check on the Congress in a system that has many checks and balances.

Congressional Power to Enact Laws

The U.S. Constitution may be the most important source of law in the United States, but the laws enacted by Congress are also very important. The laws created by Congress, also known as statutes, must be consistent with the Constitution. Because the people are the source of the power in this nation, and the Constitution is a delegation of that power to the government, any attempt to create a law that goes beyond the Constitution's delegation takes power from the people. Such a law is said to be unconstitutional, and it cannot be enforced.

One of the most significant areas in which Congress creates laws is the area of interstate commerce. The Interstate Commerce clause of the Constitution has been read very broadly, and Congress often uses it to create laws covering a very wide range of our daily lives. The Constitution specifically grants to Congress the power to regulate commerce between the states. Curiously enough, this power has been the source of many of our laws that address issues of discrimination and equal employment opportunity. Because discrimination can have an impact on interstate commerce, Congress has the power to require employers to comply with laws that prohibit the making of employment-related decisions based on an employee's race, color, sex, religion, national origin, age, or handicapping condition. We will discuss employment discrimination later, but it is important to remember that just as these laws are derived from the power of Congress to regulate interstate commerce, so too Congress must have a constitutionally derived power in order to create any law.

Executive Power to Regulate and Enforce

The President, as the chief executive, has the power to create regulations through various agencies in the executive branch of the federal government. Because the President is the chief executive of the government, the President has the responsibility of overseeing all the administrative agencies of the government. These agencies include the Departments of Defense, Treasury, Interior, Education, and many others. The regulations created to administer these agencies to a great extent determine how the laws created by Congress are put into effect.

For example, Congress may create a broad statement of law that generally prohibits employers from discriminating against employees based on race. The Department of Labor might then be the administrative agency designated to create detailed regulations to achieve this objective. These regulations are given the same force and effect as law, and are followed by courts in deciding whether an employer is guilty of employment discrimination.

It is important to remember that the President tells the administrative agencies what policies should be emphasized. The regulations and activities of the agencies generally reflect the philosophy of the President. However, Congress retains the power to create a law that is specific, not merely a general statement of law. It thereby ultimately retains the power to accomplish specific objectives.

Executive Power to Order

The President also has the power to create executive orders. Such orders have the force and effect of law. For example, President Nixon ordered that businesses which had contracts with the government would be required to engage in programs of "affirmative action" to give racial minorities a special hiring status, thereby increasing the number of minorities hired by these employers. The executive order can be used by the President to address many problems, but it is still subordinate to a constitutional statute enacted by Congress. (We have been talking about federal law generally. However, state laws are formed in much the same manner.)

Where Does the Law Come From?

Distribution of power via the Constitution
Congressional power to enact laws
Executive power to regulate and enforce
Executive power to order

Memory Testers

1. True/False. The President of the United States has the power to make laws.

2. True/False. Congress can create regulations to enforce laws which it has previously enacted.

3. True/False. Regulations issued by the executive branch of government in response to a Congressional statute have less power than the statute itself.

4. True/False. Congress enforces its own laws.

5. True/False. The U.S. Constitution gives specific powers to the states, but anything else is reserved for the Congress.

6. True/False. The U.S. Constitution gives power to the states.

Memory Tester Discussion

1. False.   The President has the power to issue orders but not to make laws. Executive orders are subordinate to a statute or law enacted by Congress.

2. False.   Congress enacts laws, but the executive branch develops regulations for enforcement and enforces laws. The federal courts have the task of determining if a given law is constitutional, but neither passes laws nor enforces them.

3. False.   Regulations issued by the executive branch in response to a law or statute passed by Congress will have the full force of law once they are adopted by Congress. Title IX, discussed in Chapter 13, is a good example of a law being passed by Congress, followed by the creation of regulations by the executive branch, followed by the adoption of those regulations by Congress, thus giving the regulations the force of law.

4. False.   Congress does not have the power to enforce its own laws. Only the executive branch can enforce laws passed by Congress.

5. False.   Actually, it's the other way around. The states gave the federal government specific powers. Anything else is reserved for the states.

6. False.   The people are the source of the power and through the Constitution have given a portion of that power to the federal government. Whenever the federal government enacts a law which tries to take more power from the people than the people have given via the Constitution, the law is unconstitutional, although might not be so declared until the judiciary acts.

Memory Testers—Short Answer

1. What are four reasons why society has laws?
2. Discuss and give an example which illustrates the statement "Our rights as citizens are extensive, but they are limited by the law so that we may realize the greatest degree of freedom consistent with the freedom of our fellow citizens."

Additional Reading

The study of the source of law is intertwined with history, sociology, and political tides. For more information on the topic, you might want to look at some of these classic references:

Cardozo, Benjamin N. (1921). *The Nature of the Judicial Process*. New Haven, CT: Yale University Press.

Friedman, Lawrence Meir. (1984). *American Law*. New York: W.W. Norton Co.

Holmes, Oliver Wendell. (1923). *The Common Law*. Boston: Little, Brown and Co.

Pound, Roscoe. (1922). *An Introduction to the Philosophy of Law*. New Haven, CT: Yale University Press.

Wormser, R. A. (1962). *The Story of the Law*. New York: Simon and Schuster.

Chapter 2

The Structure of Our Legal System: How It Works

Jurisdiction is the key to understanding our legal system. Jurisdiction refers both to geographic areas and to topics within the law.

Federal Jurisdiction

Federal courts have jurisdiction over cases involving federal topics or subject matter and disputes between two states. Except for special access, referred to as "diversity," provided to the federal courts on the basis of the states of residence of the parties, the jurisdiction of federal courts is not available to most types of cases found in sports-related lawsuits except those alleging a violation of constitutional rights such as equal protection, due process, or specific federal laws such as Title IX, Title VII, or the Equal Pay Act. Indeed, the statement "I'll take it all the way to the Supreme Court" is not a promise that can be fulfilled in most cases.

The United States is divided into several geographic federal judicial districts. Lawsuits over which the federal judicial system has jurisdiction and which arise within a particular district are heard by the federal court for that district. Whatever decision is made serves as a precedent only within that district. Although it seems that each district would arrive at the same decision if faced with the same facts, it just isn't so. In fact, often one district will have decided a particular issue directly opposite the decision on a similar case in another district. So when you read a news report about a court case, don't jump to apply it as a precedent ("rule") in your situation unless it was decided in your district. Even then, a decision can be changed by appeal.

What Federal District Is Yours?

First: Maine, Massachusetts, New Hampshire, Rhode Island

Second: Vermont, New York, Connecticut

Third: Pennsylvania, New Jersey, Delaware

Fourth: West Virginia, Virginia, Maryland, North Carolina, South Carolina

Fifth: Texas, Louisiana, Mississippi

Sixth: Michigan, Ohio, Kentucky, Tennessee

Seventh: Wisconsin, Illinois, Indiana

Eighth: North Dakota, South Dakota, Minnesota, Iowa, Nebraska, Missouri, Arkansas

Ninth: Washington, Idaho, Montana, Oregon, California, Nevada, Arizona, Alaska, Hawaii

Tenth: Wyoming, Utah, Colorado, Kansas, Oklahoma, New Mexico

A plaintiff or defendant who believes an error has been made in the court's procedures can appeal the decision to the next higher court. An appeal is based on an alleged procedural problem with the application of law such as a potential witness erroneously not being allowed to testify by the judge. An appeal cannot be based on the fact that the losing party simply doesn't like to lose. In the case of federal courts, the decision of the District Court is appealed to the Court of Appeals. The Court of Appeals does not retry the case; the witnesses are not asked to testify again. Instead the written record of the case, written briefs based on it, and short oral arguments by the attorneys are reviewed by the Court of Appeals to see if the alleged procedural irregularities occurred and, if they did, to see if they affected the outcome.

Then, if one side or the other still thinks legal fairness has been denied, they may apply to the next and last level, the U.S. Supreme Court. The Supreme Court receives many more applications than it agrees to review. If the Supreme Court refuses to review the case, the decision by the Court of Appeals is permanent and everyone goes home. If the Supreme Court agrees to review the case, the Supreme Court will review the written record from the lower courts and written briefs prepared by each side's attorney. Additionally, the Court will usually hear oral arguments by the attorneys. The Supreme Court's final decision now becomes precedent for the entire United States.

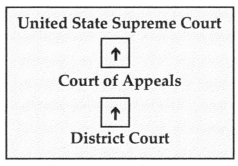

So until a case involving a particular question is finally reviewed by the Supreme Court of the United States, no one can be certain how the question will be decided or what the "rule" is. For instance, cases involving the constitutionality of the National Collegiate Athletic Association's drug testing program have been decided by lower courts, but no case has yet found its way to the Supreme Court. Until one does, we will remain unsure if the drug testing program is constitutional or unconstitutional. Even though news reports of the

INTERIM REVIEW

Federal Subject Matter Jurisdiction

Subject matter jurisdiction of federal courts extends to:

- federal laws
- constitutional issues
- disagreements between states and other situations (not of particular importance in sports law), such as diversity of citizenship among parties, treaties, and so on

Precedent value of federal courts applies to:

- the district in which the district court is located
- the entire United States if the decision is from the U.S. Supreme Court

federal district court decisions may be interesting, we should remember that the absolutely final word on federal constitutionality has not been heard until we hear from the Supreme Court.

State Jurisdiction

Most lawsuits involving sport situations are not within the jurisdiction of the federal courts but instead are found in the state court systems. Although the various states name their courts differently, the process of appeal and the impact of precedents remain the same.

When a student who has broken an arm in a physical education class begins a lawsuit on the basis of negligence, the lawsuit will usually be tried in the first level state court. Some states call that first level court the Supreme Court or Court of Common Pleas. Others call it the Superior Court. Whatever its name, the losers can appeal the decision to the next higher state court *if* they can find something in the record which they identify as being sufficiently procedurally unfair.

For instance, in New York, a negligence claim for $10,000 or more is first heard in the Supreme Court. If an appeal of the New York State Supreme Court's decision is made, the appeal is heard by the Appellate Division of the Supreme Court. If an appeal from the Appellate Division's decision is made, the appeal then goes to the highest court in New York, the New York State Court of Appeals. Whatever the Court of Appeals decides is the final word. Unless a federal question or some other point of federal jurisdiction is involved, the case cannot be appealed out of the state and into the federal courts.

Precedents

Is a decision in someone else's lawsuit important in your case? The answer depends on where the other case was decided.

The notion of precedent is important in American law. Past judicial decisions form a body of legal opinion called case law. When a particular issue has been decided by means of a lawsuit, the decision joins the body of case law. If another case comes to court involving the same or similar facts, the previously decided case will be used to provide direction on how the new case should be decided. This use of previous decisions to give direction to new decisions is what is meant by "precedent." Additionally, a past case serving as a precedent for a current one provides a helpful guide, not just for the judge but for all of us who might face the same set of circumstances. However, not all previous cases serve as precedents.

Within your state, if a case is settled out of court it has absolutely no precedent value. That means that if the plaintiff receives a cash settlement for a broken arm caused by the teacher placing a chair under the basketball backboard, the case has *not* established a rule that similar circumstances would yield a verdict of negligence. Out-of-court settlements have no value as precedents because the questions involved in the case are not actually decided by a court. The parties have just gotten together and decided who pays what to whom. Sometimes out-of-court settlements have little to do with who was at fault but rather simply mean that the defendant believes it would be more expensive and perhaps riskier to go to court.

Within your state, if the court reached a verdict in a case, it has precedent value but only within the geographic jurisdiction of the court. If a county court arrived at a decision, cases with similar facts in the same county might find that the first case serves as a precedent for them but cases outside the county would not.

What's the effect of finding a case that has precedent value? If the facts involved in your case are similar and if it is being tried in the same jurisdiction, a case that serves as precedent *guides* the court's decision in your case. However, that doesn't mean that your case must turn out the same as the precedent case. For instance, an attorney might be able to "distinguish" your case from the precedent case by pointing out some facts or circumstances that make it sufficiently dissimilar so that the logic of the first case won't apply. Or the court may decide that the rule formed by the precedent case should no longer be a rule.

An example of this second situation is found in *Rutter v. Northeastern Beaver County School District* (437 A 2nd 1198 [1981]). The assumption of risk defense (discussed in Chapters 6 and 14) to a claim of negligence used to be about the same in Pennsylvania as in other states. There were cases decided previously that served as precedents for deciding the issue of assumption of risk. However, the court's decision in *Rutter* indicated a change of mind. New definitions for some of the required elements were established in *Rutter* that resulted in the assumption of risk defense becoming almost impossible to use effectively in Pennsylvania. Thus *Rutter* became a new precedent and overruled earlier cases that had served previously as precedents.

Don't treat the idea of precedent lightly. You need to understand when a case applies to you and when it doesn't. Often we will read about a lawsuit that is apparently earthshaking for our profession. For example, a number of articles and talks have discussed the impact of the Seattle case (*Thompson et al. v. Seattle Public School District No. 1 et al.* Court of Appeals, Div. 1, Washington. No. 11579-1-I [1983]) on our programs. We have been told that, because of the Seattle case, we now need to show our athletes films of injuries so they *really understand* what risks they are taking when they participate in sports. In the name of the Seattle case, some of us have developed multi-page descriptive risk statements for our students to sign. Certainly, having our students understand the risks involved helps them concentrate on safety and is also a good idea for other reasons.

But the truth is that the Seattle case, a case involving football player Chris Thompson, who was catastrophically injured by using an improper tackling technique, has no precedent value. It has no precedent value even in the state of Washington. Its lack of precedent value is because it was settled out of court before a decision on the merits was made by the Court of Appeals. If, instead of being settled out of court, the appeal had been completed by the court, the case would have had potential precedent value within Washington, but not elsewhere. So take headlines with a grain of salt and a large dose of good background knowledge of legal issues.

Mechanics of a Lawsuit

We've talked about the impact of a case's value as precedent, and we've talked about jurisdiction and the difference between state and federal judicial systems. But once a case gets to court, how is a decision made?

Elements

The legal theory used in a particular case determines what elements need to be proven. The term "elements" refers to the minimum points for which evidence must be offered by the plaintiff. For instance, a claim of negligence requires the plaintiff (injured

INTERIM REVIEW

Precedent

When a court case is used to tout a particular point, as has been the situation with the Seattle case, be careful. Ask yourself:

1. Does the case have precedent value for me in my state? The answer will be "no" if the case was settled out of court and also "no" if the court's decision was in a jurisdiction of an other state.

2. Even if there is no precedent value, does the issue merit consideration in a professional sense? If so, don't hesitate to consider the issue but consider it without the "hype" or sense of legal urgency created by the erroneous belief that the par ticular case mandates a change.

It is also important to remember that a decision made in a lower court might be appealed. So even if the lower court's decision is made in your state and thus has precedent value, a successful appeal might radically change the precedent. As a friend of Casey Stengel said, "It's not over 'til it's over."

person) to present evidence supporting each of the four elements of *duty, breach, cause,* and *harm*. If no evidence is offered for any one of the four elements, the defendant can ask the judge to declare a "summary judgment" or a "compulsory nonsuit." Summary judgment and compulsory nonsuit are fancy terms meaning that the plaintiff's case is thrown out of court with prejudice. "Prejudice" means that the case cannot be brought back to the court later.

So the plaintiff must offer evidence in the form of testimony (verbal or documentary) supporting each element. The jury then decides if the evidence is believable. Thus, the jury is sometimes referred to as the "trier of fact." The "trier of law" is the judge. The judge is the one who has the responsibility of deciding if the technical requirements have been met.

Standard of Certainty

In a civil trial such as one dealing with issues of negligence or breach of contract, the jury uses the standard of certainty, defined as a "preponderance of the evidence." This concept might be described by the word picture of a scale laden with the believable evidence. If the plaintiff's believable evidence is more than 50 percent persuasive for each of the required elements, the jury should bring forth a judgment of guilty against the defendant.

In a criminal trial (theft, criminal battery, etc.), the jury uses the standard of certainty usually defined as "beyond a reasonable doubt." This standard is much more difficult to meet than the civil trial's preponderance of the evidence standard. This is as it should be. After all, a civil trial usually involves only money whereas a criminal trial may involve going to jail. Beyond a reasonable doubt does not mean "beyond a shadow of a doubt," nor does it mean "in all certainty." The key is the word "reasonable."

Another, intermediate, standard of certainty is used in some states' appeals processes. It is more than a preponderance and less than beyond a reasonable doubt. It is described by the words "clear and convincing evidence."

Burden of Proof

In a civil trial the plaintiff must carry the burden of proving the required elements by a preponderance of the evidence. In a criminal trial the prosecuting attorney must carry the burden of proving the required elements beyond a reasonable doubt. Theoretically, if the burden of proof is not met, the defendant does not need to present any evidence at all because our judicial system is founded on the premise that the defendant is innocent until proven guilty.

In a few special circumstances in civil cases, the burden of proof can be shifted to the defendant. However, because this only happens in very unusual situations, we won't discuss the possibility more than just to mention its existence.

Conceptual and Contextual Subdivisions in Law

Constitutional law, contract law, criminal law, administrative law, property law, and tort law are all major *conceptual* divisions created to make it easier to delineate particular concepts. Education law and sports law are terms that do *not* delineate concepts but rather draw from all the areas of the law. Sports law and education law are terms that indicate *contextual* circumstances (e.g., schools or sporting situations), and the legal concepts for sports law and education law are drawn from all the conceptual subdivisions.

For instance, a teacher's hiring involves contract law; a coach's search of an athlete's locker involves constitutional law; a student's broken arm involves tort law; and the rental of a gymnasium involves property law. Indeed, education law and sports law are two contextual areas involving the entire range of the law.

The Anatomy of a Case

It might be useful about now to take a look at an actual case to see its progression through the legal system. You can find this case through the legal reporters in your nearby law library, if access is available, or through the internet.

The decision and the court's reasoning for many cases, particularly in the appellate system and the federal court system, are printed and available to the public soon after the decision is made. Those bookcases you see standing behind lawyers on television are full of legal reporters. Legal reporters are not journalists who have the courthouse as their beat; legal reporters are books full of a particular court's decisions. Most of the decisions found in the legal reporters include such details as the facts and allegations, a summary of applicable law and precedents, the decisions in the lower courts (courts which have previously heard the case), and the current court's rationale for its decision.

The case we're going to look at is *Smith v. NCAA*. The citation is *NCAA v. Smith*. No. 98-84, Supreme Court of the United States, 525 U.S. 84; 119 S. Ct. 924; 142 L. Ed. 2d 929. The case was decided on February 23, 1999. If you can't find an appropriate set of legal reporters, try finding the case through the internet. An easily accessible internet site to use is http://www.law.cornell.edu.

The citation tells us a lot about the case. For instance, the notations: "525 U.S. 84; 119 S. Ct. 924; 142 L. Ed. 2d 929" tell us we will find the decision printed in several different legal reports: volume 525 of U.S. Reports at page 84, volume 119 of the Supreme Court Reports at page 924, and volume 142 of the second series of the Lawyer's Edition at page 929. The notation No. 98-84 tells us that the case was argued as part of the 1998 term of the Supreme Court and that its tracking number for the court was 84. If you have access to an academic library, it might be interesting to look at some of the newspaper accounts of the issues in the case. With the decision date in hand, you can easily do that because the *NCAA v. Smith* case found its way into the legal press as well as newspapers.

The Supreme Court uses the term, "syllabus" to mean a brief summary of the issues in the case. Other courts use terms other than syllabus, but you'll always find some sort of brief background statement regarding the case which brings you up-to-date for the decision of the current court. The Supreme Court also tells us what its decision is. In the pages following the syllabus is the court's rationale for its decision and, if necessary and appropriate, the rationale from those members of the court who disagreed in whole or in part with the majority's decision. In the *NCAA v. Smith* case, the decision was unanimous, so there is no dissenting opinion.

Let's take a look at just the syllabus portion of the *NCAA v. Smith* decision:

> National Collegiate Athletic Association. Petitioner v. R. M. Smith, Respondent[1] on writ of *certiorari*[2] to the United States Court of Appeals for the Third Circuit. Justice Ginsburg delivered the opinion[3] of the Court.

Note 1: Smith sued the NCAA, not the other way around, so normally Smith's name would be first. However, it is the NCAA which is appealing (petitioning) a lower court's decision, so for this portion of the case's trek to completion, the NCAA name appears first and Smith is called the respondent because she is responding to the NCAA's appeal.

Note 2: Also, the term, "writ of certiorari" refers to a request for the Supreme Court to hear the case. If certiorari is not granted, the court will not hear the case and the lower court's decision stands. In this case, certiorari was given, thus the Supreme court heard the case.

Note 3: One justice usually has the responsibility of writing the winning opinion. If there are justices who don't agree with the reasoning or with the outcome, they can write separate opinions. This case was decided unanimously, so there is only one opinion written.

> This case concerns the amenability of the NCAA (or Association) to a private action under Title IX of the Education Amendments of 1972. The NCAA is an unincorporated association of approximately 1,200 members, including virtually all public and private universities and four-year colleges conducting major athletic programs

in the United States; the Association serves to maintain intercollegiate athletics as an integral part of its members' educational programs. Title IX proscribes sex discrimination in "any education program or activity receiving federal financial assistance." 20 U.S.C. sec. 1681(a).[4]

> *Note 4: 20 U.S.C. sec. 1681(a) is the statutory reference for the law called Title IX. Smith couldn't just say, "The NCAA is unfair." She needed to find a law which says it is illegal to be unfair in the way she is alleging the NCAA was unfair. That law is Title IX.*

The complainant in this case, Renee M. Smith, sued the NCAA under Title IX alleging that the Association discriminated against her on the basis of her sex by denying her permission to play intercollegiate volleyball at federally assisted institutions. Reversing the District Court's refusal to allow Smith to amend[5] her *pro se*[6] complaint, the Court of Appeals for the Third Circuit held that the NCAA's receipt of dues[7] from federally funded member institutions would suffice to bring the Association within the scope of Title IX. We reject[8] that determination as inconsistent with the governing statute, regulation, and this Court's decisions. Dues payments from recipients of federal funds, we hold, do not suffice to render the dues recipient subject to Title IX. We do not address alternative ground, urged by respondent and the United States as *amicus curiae*,[9] in support of Title IX's application to the NCAA in this litigation, and leave resolution of those grounds to the courts below on remand.[10]

> *Note 5: Smith asked permission to fix her lawsuit's formal papers (complaint) to add the missing material.*
>
> *Note 6: Pro se means by herself. Initially Smith, the plaintiff, filed her lawsuit against the NCAA without an attorney doing the work for her.*
>
> *Note 7: One of the three required elements for which evidence must be offered in order to charge a defendant with a violation of Title IX is that the defendant receives federal funding. If any of the required elements is missing, it is impossible for a plaintiff to win. So a defendant can point out that a required element is totally missing and ask the judge to throw the case out of court (dismiss it) because it is impossible to be won. The district court (first level court in the federal system) agreed with the NCAA and dismissed the case.*

> *Note 8: The Court of Appeals didn't agree with the district court and reversed the decision in the lower court.*
>
> *Note 9: Smith, as well as the NCAA, had help from various amicae curiae briefs. An* amicus curiae *brief is a written argument from a "friend of the court" who has an opinion about how a particular issue should be decided and wants the court to hear it.*
>
> *Note 10: The U.S. Supreme Court disagreed with the Court of Appeals about dues but sent (remanded) the case back to the lower court for more proceedings. For instance, if Smith is successful upon remand, in her argument not addressed by the Supreme Court, that the NCAA, through its relationship with the federally-funded National Youth Sports Program, receives federal money, she would be able to bring the NCAA within the jurisdiction of Title IX.*

So the *NCAA v. Smith* case illustrates the appeal process and the use of *amicus curiae* briefs. It is a significant case in that its outcome can have a great impact on issues of gender equity. Perhaps by the time you read this, the remanded case will have been decided. Why not check via the legal reporters or the internet?

What's in a Word?

Now that we've taken a brief view of how the legal system works, it might be helpful to review some frequently used terms before we go on to discuss the concept of legal fault in Chapter 3.

Adversary: The plaintiff and defendants in a trial are adversaries or opponents.

Amicus: An *amicus curiae* is a friend of the court. Often when a case is being appealed, nonparties may have a strong interest in the outcome and therefore offer a written argument known as a "brief" to the court.

Appeal: At the conclusion of the first trial, a party who is dissatisfied with all or part of the outcome can appeal the decision to a higher court if sufficient grounds for appeal can be found. Grounds for appeal are generally procedural errors made by the judge in the first trial.

Appellate: This term is an adjective which is used to describe a court which is hearing an appeal or the appeals court's decision in the case, as in "appellate decision."

Beyond a reasonable doubt: This is the standard of certainty required in order to be found guilty of a crime.

Breach: When someone owes a duty to someone else such as in a contract, but fails to perform correctly, that person has breached the duty. A breach which relates to contractual duties may lead to a lawsuit for a breach of contract. A breach which relates to the failure to appropriately fulfill the duty to protect someone from the foreseeable risk of unreasonable harm, such as exists between a teacher and a student, may lead to a lawsuit for negligence.

Brief: A brief is a written argument which is submitted to the court concerning the issues in a particular case.

Burden of proof: This phrase refers to the obligation of providing evidence to prove a particular element. Almost without exception, the plaintiff has the burden of proof.

Cause of action: The legal theory under which someone files a lawsuit is the cause of action. Breach of contract, negligence, defamation, and a violation of Title IX are all examples of causes of action.

Certiorari: When someone wants the U.S. Supreme Court to hear an appeal from a decision in a lower court, the court is asked to certify that it is willing to hear the case. The court receives many more requests than it can hear, so in the majority of cases, it denies the certification. The term *certiorari* refers to the certification or denial of certification to hear the case.

Civil: A civil case never involves a jail sentence. It is not a crime. Rather, a civil case refers to those behaviors and duties we owe to other members of society. They are not the product of legislative action but rather the product of acceptable behavior within society.

Clear and convincing evidence: This phrase refers to the intermediate standard of certainty required in most appeals. The standard is not routinely used at levels below the appeal.

Compulsory nonsuit: Compulsory nonsuit is the same thing as summary judgment. Different states use different terms.

Constitutionality: Legislative action must only involve those actions over which a particular legislative body has power granted to it by the constitution. If the legislative body acts within that power, its law is likely to be constitutional. If it exceeds its constitutionally granted power, the law may be found to be unconstitutional by the judiciary. Remember, the legislature makes the laws but the judiciary interprets them.

Criminal: When someone performs an act prohibited by law that person has committed a crime. Crimes and their punishments are specifically spelled out in statutes. If there is no statute, there is no crime.

Damages: The amount of money the plaintiff is suing for or receives at the end of the trial is called damages. Damages can be compensatory, in which case they are intended to recompense the plaintiff for the injury suffered or money lost because of the defendant's wrongdoing. Damages can also be punitive, in which case they are intended to punish the defendant beyond the requirement of making compensation to the plaintiff. Punitive damages are intended to send a message to the defendant and those in similar situationsthat such misdeeds will not be tolerated by society.

Decision: When a court hears the evidence, it determines an outcome of a lawsuit.The outcome of the lawsuit is the decision.

Defendant: The defendant is the party accused of wrongdoing.

Dissent: When a lawsuit is heard by a panel of judges, such as occurs at the Supreme Court, there are times when the judges do not agree on what the decision should be. In this situation, the majority rules. However, the judges who disagree may choose to write an opinion which explains why they disagree; this opinion is the dissent.

Distinguish: Precedents, cases which have been previously decided which might influence the current case, are powerful in determining legal points. If one side of the case, either plaintiff or defendant, wants to nullify the potential power of a precedent case, that party would try to distinguish it from the case currently in the court. To distinguish means to point out how the two cases are dissimilar, making the precedent case not applicable to the case being litigated.

Elements: Each type of lawsuit has specific requirements for which evidence must be presented by the plaintiff. The term "elements" is another way of referring to the requirements.

Error: An error is a procedural mistake, which if significant might provide grounds for an appeal by the losing party.

Evidence: Evidence is any material or statement which is offered in court to prove a point. Evidence is not always accurate, nor is it always truthful. The credibility of evidence is what is being weighed by the trier of fact (jury in a jury trial).

Holding: The decision in a trial is the holding.

Independent contractor: An independent contractor is a person who makes a contract to perform a job but retains the power to determine when and how the job will be performed. An independent contractor is *not* an employee. An employee is under greater control and direction by the employer. The difference between independent contractors and employees is of significance in negligence cases as well as workers' compensation and taxation cases.

Judgment: When the court makes a final decision, it is sometimes referred to as a judgment. Sometimes the phrase "I have a judgment against the defendant" will be used to indicate that the court found the defendant guilty in a civil trial. "Judgment proof" is another often-used phrase. "Judgment proof" means that even if the defendant is found guilty, the defendant has no money, so the plaintiff wins but loses anyway.

Lower court: The first court that tries a case is called the lower court. If the case is appealed, the case goes to a higher court for review.

Malpractice: When someone fails to perform a duty correctly, malpractice occurs. The term is sometimes used to denote specific situations in which negligence might have occurred, such as in medical malpractice.

Moot: Sometimes a court will rule that it would not be appropriate to render adecision in a case because the circumstances surrounding the case have changed since the case was filed in ways which would make the decision pointless. For instance, if a potential student who has filed a lawsuit alleging discrimination in the denial of a college admission graduates from that college before the court has reached its decision, the outcome of the case might be determined to be moot or pointless.

Motion: A motion is a formal request for a particular action or decision made to the judge by a party's attorney.

Parties: The defendant(s) and plaintiff(s) are the only parties in a lawsuit. A party must have an interest in the outcome of the case.

Petitioner: The petitioner is the person who appeals a decision made by a lower court by petitioning a higher court to review it.

Plaintiff: The plaintiff is the party complaining of some sort of injury.

Precedent: Previously decided cases in the highest court in the same jurisdiction involving the same general facts and legal issues may provide guidance to the current court in its decision making.

Prejudice: In the sense this term is used in this book, it refers to a court decision prohibiting the losing plaintiff from having another chance to bring the same lawsuit to court. For instance, when summary judgment is granted, it is usually granted with prejudice, thus barring the plaintiff from repairing the case and returning to court.

Preponderance of the evidence: This is the standard of certainty required in order to be found guilty of a civil wrong.

Pro se: When plaintiffs file suits by themselves, without help from an attorney, they are working *pro se*, by themselves.

Regulation: Once a legislative body such as Congress has passed a law, the executive branch will create regulations that spell out the details of the law's implementation. Regulations have the force of law.

Remanded: When an appellate court sends a case back to a lower court for more work or proceedings, it remands the case. Usually the case is remanded with specific directions about what the lower court is supposed to consider.

Remedy: The plaintiff asks for something in a lawsuit. The plaintiff may ask for a remedy of money to replace lost salary, pay doctor bills, or soothe pain and suffering. The plaintiff may ask for a remedy of job reinstatement in a lawsuit involving firing. The remedy is whatever the plaintiff is asking for and/or whatever the victorious plaintiff receives.

Respondent: The party who is responding to the other party's appeal is the respondent.

Settled: When a court decides a case, a judgment, verdict, or decision is made. When a case is settled, it means that a final judgment, verdict, or decision was not made, but rather the parties to the case reached an agreement before the court finished its work. Settled cases have no precedent value.

Standard of care: When a duty is owed to another, the standard of care is a term of art which indicates how carefully the person needs to be when carrying out the duty owed. Negligence cases often involve the issue of whether the defendant met the standard of care. The phrase, "reasonable, prudent, up-to-date person, coach or teacher" is one which relates to the standard of care provided the person to whom the duty is owed. Professional standards are often used to create a presumption about the level or standard of care one party owes another.

Statute of limitations: Civil wrongs and a few crimes have prescribed statutes of limitations. For instance, in most states the statute of limitation for defamation is quite short, often only one year. This means that unless a plaintiff formally files a lawsuit within one year, the case cannot be won if the defendant claims the statute as a defense. The various time limits are set by laws within each state.

Sui juris: Children may testify in a trial if they are *sui juris*, a term that refers to the child's ability to know what right and wrong are and to know the importance of telling the truth. Various states have different ages at which a child is presumed *sui juris* and non-*sui juris*. In addition, the judge will often interview a young potential witness to decide if the particular witness-to-be understands right and wrong.

Summary judgment: When the plaintiff has failed to present even some amount of significant evidence to support one or more of the required elements, the defendant's attorney may file a motion for summary judgment. If granted by the judge, the plaintiff's case is thrown out of court with prejudice.

Syllabus: Decisions from the U.S. Supreme Court include a brief overview of the case's issues, its history, and the outcome known as the syllabus.

Term of art: Some words and phrases have special meaning which might not be apparent if only reviewed in their normal, non-legal usage. When this is the case, it is said that the word or phrase is a term of art, thus the hearer or reader should know that special meaning is attached.

Tolling: When a minor is injured, it would be unfair to apply the normal statute of limitations. A 5-year-old child wouldn't understand enough about the judicial system to know when a lawsuit should be filed. Of course the parents are often allowed to file a lawsuit on behalf of the youngster but the courts realize that when the parents don't file, it would be unfair to bar the child from court later. So the statute of limitations is tolled for minors. That means that the clock is stopped until later. Some states allow the minor until a year, or after the minor becomes an adult, to file a lawsuit. When we start cleaning out our old files, we need to remember that the concept of tolling exists. Records of an accident that occurred a number of years ago may still be needed if the injured child files a lawsuit upon becoming an adult.

Tort: In the legal sense, a tort is a civil rather than criminal wrong. Examples of specific torts are negligence, defamation, civil battery, and so on.

Trier of fact: The jury weighs the believability of the evidence and decides which evidence is fact.

Trier of law: The judge makes all decisions that involve the legal requirements of the case.

Writ of *certiorari*: See *Certiorari* on page 23.

Memory Testers

1. True/False. The parties to a lawsuit include the judge, jury, plaintiff, and defendant.
2. True/False. The defendant is the person or entity accused of wrongdoing and the plaintiff is the injured person or entity.
3. True/False. A tort is a crone.
4. True/False. The burden of proof falls on the defendant to prove innocence.
5. True/False. In most states a civil case requires a standard of certainty described as a preponderance of the evidence.
6. True/False. A criminal case requires a standard of certainty described as beyond a shadow of a doubt.

7. True/False. Sports law involves concepts peculiar to sport situations.

8. True/False. A civil case involving the negligence of a physical education teacher can be appealed ultimately to the U.S. Supreme Court.

9. True/False. A case that has been decided by a state's highest court may serve as a precedent within the state but not in other states.

10. True/False. A defendant who loses has just as much right to appeal a case as a plaintiff who loses.

11. True/False. Evidence for each element of a claim must be presented by the plaintiff or else the judge may declare summary judgment or compulsory non-quit.

12. True/False. A court named "Court of Appeals" is less likely to have witnesses on the stand than the court named "Court of Common Pleas."

13. True/False. In order to be considered proof, evidence must be written and signed rather than being verbal.

14. True/False. In a jury trial, the "trier of fact" and the "trier of law" are not the same.

Memory Tester Discussion

1. False.   The term "parties" only includes those people who have an interest in the outcome of the lawsuit. The parties would be the plaintiff(s) and the defendant(s). The judge and jury have no stake in the case's outcome, so they are not parties.

2. True.   The plaintiff is the party who is complaining and who has initiated the lawsuit.

3. False.   A tort is a civil wrong, not a criminal wrong. The term is used as a generic term for such things as negligence, defamation, trespass, and so on. Because a tort is a civil rather than a criminal wrong, if you are found guilty of a tort you do not go to jail.

4. False.   The plaintiff has the burden of proving all the required elements of a particular case. Our judicial

system is based on the premise that a defendant is innocent until proven guilty.

5. True.   The standard of certainty is lower in a civil case than in a criminal case.

6. False. The jury in a criminal trial doesn't have to be absolutely, positively certain the defendant is guilty. On the other hand, the jury must be more sure than in civil trials. So, rather than the standard of beyond a shadow of a doubt, the high, but more realistic, beyond a reasonable doubt standard is used in criminal trials.

7. False. Sports law draws from all areas of the law. It includes, among others, issues in property, contract, tort, and constitutional law. Sports law refers to the context of sport rather than the conceptual area of sport as a legal entity.

8. False. The U.S. Supreme Court is the highest federal court, but because it is a federal court, it would not have subject matter jurisdiction over a negligence case. Negligence does not involve a federal or constitutional question.

9.   True. When the state's highest court decides a case, the case may serve as precedent for cases within that court's jurisdiction until a similar case is decided differentlyby the highest court.

10. True. If grounds for an appeal exist, it makes no difference whether the defendant or plaintiff is dissatisfied with the decision. Either may appeal an adverse decision.

11. True. The plaintiff has the obligation to present evidence for each element. If the plaintiff fails to do so, the judge has the option of granting the defendant's motion for summary judgment or compulsory non-quit. The judge rather than the jury makes this particular decision because it involves a matter of law (e.g., has the plaintiff presented some evidence for each element?) instead of a matter of fact (e.g., did the witness who testified about an element tell the truth?). Remember, the judge is the trier of law and the jury is the trier of fact.

12. True.   Courts that are deciding appeals rely mainly on the written record of the first trial, written briefs (arguments) filed by each party's attorneys, and oral argument also made by the attorneys. Witnesses are not recalled to testify at the court hearing the appeal.

13. False.   Evidence can be anything from spoken testimony to written records to urine test results. The jury considers the weight and believability of the evidence. For instance, in a contractual dispute, a signed contract is likely to carry more weight than verbal testimony contradicting the signed contract. In a very real sense then, everything spoken or presented in court is evidence, not proof. The jury decides if the evidence or any combination of the evidence actually proves an element to the required standard of certainty.

14. True.   The judge is the trier of law and the jury is the trier of fact. Only in a nonjury trial will the judge be both the trier of the law and the trier of the fact.

Memory Tester—Short Answer Question

1. Earlier in this chapter we talked about an assumption of risk case in Pennsylvania named *Rutter*. What can you learn from its citation reference?

Answer: The first number, 437, indicates the volume. A2d indicates the case is found in the Atlantic Reporter, second series. Pennsylvania is one of the states whose cases are found in the Atlantic Reporter. Second series means that there is also a first series with lots of volumes containing earlier cases. 1198 is the starting page of the case and 1981 is the year of the decision in this old but interesting case.

Chapter 3
The Concept of Legal Fault:
"Who's to Blame?"

We've been taught from our very first civics lesson that we are "innocent until proven guilty." In other countries and in other times, the accused has often had to prove innocence. Proving innocence is much more difficult than proving guilt. Simply saying "I didn't do it" is not any more persuasive in the 21st century than it was 300 years ago in Salem, Massachusetts, when those accused of witchcraft proclaimed, "I am not a witch." Such a proclamation of innocence was insufficient. Instead, the accused witch had to prove innocence, and in some cases the means of proving innocence involved dying. Proving a negative, as would be required if we put the burden of proof on the accused, is often so onerous as to destroy the notion of justice.

So today, our legal system is structured in a way which puts deed to those words, "innocent until proven guilty." If we ignore the impact of the media on shaping public opinion about guilt or innocence and if we put cynicism aside, we find that at least the structure of our legal system places the burden of proof not on the accused but on the accuser.

How Is the Decision Made in a Lawsuit?

There are two things to be decided in any lawsuit: the law and the facts.

Issues of law are issues such as:

- Should a witness be able to quote the words of another? (Example: hearsay)
- Has at least some type of evidence been offered by the plaintiff supporting each of the required elements of a claim? (Example: Negligence requires four elements—duty, breach, cause, and harm.)
- Should the plaintiff's attorney be able to ask the defendant if the defendant has insurance coverage?

Issues of law are decided by the judge. That's why the judge is referred to as the trier of law. Issues of law require a knowledge of the rules and structure of our legal system, and the judge is best qualified to decide such issues.

Issues of fact are issues such as:

- Is the witness telling the truth?
- Who is more to blame for an injury?
- Was the teacher sufficiently careful to have met the teacher's standard of care?
- What amount of monetary compensation is a particular injury worth?

Issues of fact are issues that require a discernment of balance, weight, truth, motive, and such. No understanding of the law is required. Instead, an understanding of truth and lie, of human nature and community standards of behavior are needed. Therefore, the most qualified people to decide issues of fact are the members of the jury, so the jury is called the trier of fact. The judge will instruct the jury, before it begins its deliberations, on the issues of fact it is to decide. The judge will not ask the jury to decide issues of law, only issues of fact. In a nonjury trial, the judge serves as both the trier of fact and the trier of law.

Reasons for Assigning Legal Fault

Responsibility for Payment: "Why Should I Pay?"

When a young child knocks over a glass of milk or breaks a pretty dish, the first words out of the child's mouth are likely to be, "It's not my fault." The concepts of crime and punishment, action and responsibility for action, cause and effect are learned at a very early age. Indeed, parents try to teach the concepts in a child's early years so that the child begins to learn that consequences (either good or bad) follow actions. The child utters the words relating to fault in an attempt to avoid the consequences, thus letting us know that the child has already developed a basic, if not also self centered, understanding of the notion of the relationship between fault and the delivery of negative consequences.

It is not surprising then that such a basic concept as fault is adopted on a society-wide basis. In order to be an acceptable member of society, we need to bear some responsibility for our actions when those actions have an effect on some other member of society. For instance, when we are careless and that carelessness hurts someone else to whom we owed a greater level of care than we delivered, we should be held accountable. Negligence is the main legal term for that accountability.

We cannot turn the clock back. If we have injured someone, we cannot undo the injury. But society has determined that the victim of our actions should be made whole.

How can that be done if we can't undo the injury? The payment of money for damages (sometimes simply called "money damages") does not repair a broken arm, but at least it compensates for an injury in the only means possible. The money damages might pay the doctor bills. The money damages might pay for rehabilitation. The money damages might pay for time lost from work. Another term sometimes used for this type of damages is compensatory damages. The money paid is being used to compensate for the injury. So one reason for assigning legal fault is to cause the person at fault to bear the responsibility of trying to make up for actions that had a negative effect on another.

Prevention and Punishment: "Should I Change My Ways?"

Another reason for assigning legal fault is to make a point. Society hopes that if people know their actions which have negative impacts on others also have consequences on their own pocketbooks (or in the case of criminal actions, on their freedom), they will take greater care. If, in fear of having to pay damages, people take greater care, then fewer people will be injured and society as a whole is better off. Thus prevention of injury is one reason for assigning fault.

After fault has been assigned, damages can be used as punishment. The defendant is punished somewhat for a harmful action by having to pay damages. Thus the defendant may, in the future, be extra careful.

Punitive damages are damages that do not equal the value of the injury to the plaintiff but instead are intended to be a sum in addition to the amount a defendant has to pay to compensate the plaintiff for injuries. These damages are intended to hurt the defendant. Punitive damages are used only in situations in which it is important to society that the defendant and others like the defendant clearly get the message that similar behavior in the future will not be tolerated.

Punishment and prevention by fear of punishment are thought of as useful tools in creating a safer society. Sometimes they are ineffective, but currently they are the tools used.

Capacity to Bear the Loss: "Can I Afford It?"

If the person whose actions caused the negative result is not held responsible, then someone else will be. The someone else might be the injured party having to pay the doctor bills or it might be society at large having to pay the doctor bills for the plaintiff who cannot afford to do so. Although society has a bigger budget than the individual member of society, society has decided that the two people who must first face the issue of "Can I afford it?" are the plaintiff and the defendant rather than society as a whole.

If the plaintiff decides that it is better to absorb the loss than to expend money in an effort to force the defendant to pay damages, the plaintiff has decided who can afford it. On the other hand, once the plaintiff decides to try to make the defendant accountable, the courts will determine fault and then, if the defendant is at fault, decide that the defendant is the appropriate person to afford the loss rather than the plaintiff.

A person who does not want to have to afford the loss will seek, for future actions, other entities to afford it, such as insurance companies. The concept of capacity to bear the loss finds its way into other legal doctrines such as "hold harmless laws" (laws that under specific circumstances call on the school district to pay for a teacher's negligence) and the placement of caps on damages by the state for some kinds of lawsuits brought against the state (so that society as a whole will not have too big a bill).

Administrative Convenience: "Is This the Easiest Way?"

The assignment of fault allows assignment of the obligation of compensation to follow automatically and logically without having to find some other philosophical basis on which to assign the responsibility of compensating the injured party. It is clean, direct, logical, supportable, and fair.

Administratively, it allows the plaintiff to accuse and the accused to try to defend; then, if the defendant is unsuccessful, assignment of the duty of compensation without significant administrative decision making will take place. In effect, the only administrative involvement is in the provision of the forum in which to determine fault and the provision of a referee (judge) to interpret the rules.

Moral Aspects of Conduct: "Was I That Bad?"

If no one ever tells me that my behavior is inappropriate, how will I learn what is acceptable and what is not? The assignment of fault is a final grade for my behavior. It tells me that my behavior was faulty, unacceptable, uncondoned, and that it is behavior for which I bear responsibility in a negative sense. Assignment of fault helps me draw the line between acceptable behavior and unacceptable behavior. It also tells others where the line is so that they may adjust their actions accordingly.

The line between acceptable and unacceptable behavior is often changeable. The ever-expanding body of case law (past decisions) pushes the line one way or the other. What was acceptable 50 years ago may not be acceptable now. For instance, in the past the doctrine of *in loco parentis* both allowed and mandated the teacher to act as a parent in regard to students. The teacher could discipline a child as would the parent. The teacher had the responsibility of supervising as would a parent. However, case upon case has changed the doctrine so that it barely exists for college-aged students and is weaker for high school students than in the past. Each successive decision allowed society to fine-tune what is acceptable teacher behavior.

The line between acceptable and unacceptable behavior has been drawn and redrawn over the decades. The ability to redraw the line of acceptability allows the imposition of responsibility to reflect the times. It also helps the members of society to know how good they have to be in order to avoid having their behaviors found unacceptable. Assignment of fault allows society to set standards of care.

Relationships Between Defendants: "Do I Bear Some Responsibility for Another's Action?"

We are not islands unto ourselves. Instead we are tied to others in a complex set of relationships by which we can sometimes share pain, joy, obligations, and financial responsibility. In our discussion's context of assigning legal blame, there are certain relationships in which the responsibility for the actions of one person is borne by or shared by another.

When a relationship exists between defendants such as agent/principal, employee/employer, or partner/partnership, one is often legally responsible for the actions of the other. For instance, when you give someone else authority to act in your place, that person becomes your agent and you are the principal (not principal of the school). Whatever the agent does with your authority brings responsibility for consequences directly to you as the principal. As principal, you bear responsibility for the agent's actions on your behalf because you gave the agent authority to act in your place.

Coaches who unprofessionally and immorally tell players to "take the opponent's star player out of the game by any means" may be placing themselves in the position of principal (authority giver). If the athletes act as their agents and harm the opponent intentionally, the coaches may be accepting responsibility, both legal and moral, for the battery.

A situation similar to the agent/principal relationship arises in an employer/employee relationship when the employee acts in place of the employer. The legal theory of *respondent superior* comes into play in such circumstances and will allow the injured party to sue the employer as well (sometimes) as the employee. The term "*respondent superior*" indicates that the superior/boss must respond to the results of employees' actions.

"Joint and several liability" is a legal term that sometimes applies when fault has been assigned to more than one defendant. For instance, when a teacher knowingly uses dangerous facilities for a class and the supervisor either knew or should have known about the dangerous facilities but did nothing about them, both the teacher and the supervisor may be found at fault for the injuries of a student.

In many jurisdictions, defendants can be found jointly and severally liable. "Jointly and severally liable" is a legal term meaning that each defendant (in the scenario of dangerous facilities above, there were two defendants) is at fault and both (or all) are responsible for paying the plaintiff whatever damages have been awarded. Assuming that no immunity or hold harmless laws apply (immunity and hold harmless laws are discussed in Chapters 6 and 14), each defendant is

Why Determine Legal Fault?

Responsibility for payment
Prevention and punishment
Determination of capacity to bear
    the loss
Administrative convenience
Moral aspects of conduct
Identification of relationships between defendants

responsible for the total amount. If one cannot pay, the other must pay both parts.

So the assignment of fault acknowledges the existence of relationships between individuals, which may cause a somewhat remote person to bear some responsibility for the actions of another.

Memory Testers

1. True/False. The judge is the trier of fact.

2. True/False. Juries decide whether a particular witness should be allowed to testify.

3. True/False. Punitive damages are available to the plaintiff in every case.

4. True/False. If a student has been physically injured but has health/medical insurance that will pay the entire bill for the injury, the student cannot successfully sue the teacher who caused the injury because the injury has not created a financial loss.

5. True/False. The concept of punishment is only found in criminal cases, not civil cases.

6. True/False. Statutory law spells out in black and white the standard of care expected of a teacher or coach.

7. True/False. If a student sues two defendants and wins, the student will never be able to collect all the money awarded by the jury if one of the defendants has no money.

Memory Tester Discussion

1. False. The judge's responsibility is to decide issues relating to the law, not to the facts. The only time the judge carries the responsibility of weighing the facts or truthfulness of a witness' testimony is when there is no jury. But in a jury trial, the jury must determine issues of fact.

2. False. Deciding if a particular witness can testify is an issue of law, not fact. Therefore, the jury does not decide such questions. Instead, it is the responsibility of the judge to decide if the requirements of procedure are met by having a particular witness testify.

3. False. Punitive damages are allowed only in specific types of cases. Just because a plaintiff wants the defendant to be punished does not mean that the imposition of punitive damages is triggered. Compensatory damages are the damages used to compensate the plaintiff for the injury. Punitive damages are only used to punish the defendant and warn others similar to the defendant that the defendant's actions will not be tolerated.

4. False. Just because the student wisely had good health or medical insurance, the student is not precluded from suing successfully for money damages. If it were not so, the careless defendant would only fear injuring poor or uninsured plaintiffs. Instead, damages are determined by the value of the injury, pain and suffering, and so forth. Damages are not determined by the amount of the bill left unpaid because of lack of money or insurance.

5. False. Financial punishment, found in the form of punitive damages, exists in civil cases.

6. False. Case law provides a constantly developing set of standards to which the teacher or coach can look for direction concerning the standard of care required by society via its legal system. There are very few statutory standards of behavior set out for teachers and coaches. This is true because negligence law in

general depends on case law to determine the standard of care to be accepted as it reflects what the reasonable, prudent, up-to-date teacher or coach would do in similar circumstances.

7. False.   In most jurisdictions, the student would be able to collect the entire judgment from the remaining defendant. This is what happens in jurisdictions using "joint and several liability." A good example of significant change in accepted professional behavior can be seen in the old policy of some coaches to withhold water during football practice. Our profession's knowledge of heat stress has increased, and such behavior is obviously unprofessional today. For an interesting case concerning this issue, see *Mogabgab v. Orleans Parish School Board* 239 So. 2d 456 (1970).

Chapter 4
The Concept of Legal Obligation:
"Why Me?"

We owe a variety of obligations to those around us. When we earn money, we have an obligation to pay taxes to the Internal Revenue Service. When we drive a car, we owe an obligation to the pedestrians and motorists who share our streets to stop for red lights. When we teach or coach, we owe our students and athletes the duty of protecting them from foreseeable risks of unreasonable harm. We even have a duty to protect *ourselves* from foreseeable risks of unreasonable harm.

Relationships and Obligations

Generally, some type of relationship must exist in order for an obligation to exist or a duty to be owed. For instance, landlords and tenants have a relationship that involves legal obligations on both sides. The landlord must provide habitable premises and the tenant must pay rent. Employees owe an honest day's work to the employer, and the employer bears the obligation of paying the employee agreed upon wages.

Relationships Defined by the Parties

The landlord/tenant and the employer/employee relationships are of a contractual nature. Thus the specific obligations between the landlord and tenant or employer and employee are determined ahead of time by the parties to the relationship.

When an employer and employee negotiate a contract, each side of the relationship has to agree to a set of obligations. If the potential employee doesn't wish to undertake the work for the salary offered, the potential employee doesn't become an employee and no obligations develop to perform the work or to pay for the work. There is no contract, so there is no set of obligations. If the potential employer is sufficiently eager to have the work done, the potential employer can offer the potential employee more money. Thus by the negotiation process, the details of each party's obligations are developed. Once created, the existence of the contract binds the two parties to the performance of their respective obligations.

Every now and then, a relationship is formed that is initiated by the parties but defined by law. An example of this type of relationship is the employer/employee relationship found in worker's compensation law. The employer and employee establish their relationship vis-à-vis each other, but the state, through its workers' compensation laws, defines some of the obligations the employer has toward the employee.

Workers' compensation law is of particular interest in relation to the status of scholarship athletes in big-time sports at big-time athletics powerhouse colleges and universities. Both the college and the athlete would define their relationship as one of school and student, not employer and employee, but there are those who have successfully argued to the contrary in the past, both through case law and state statutes.

Workers' compensation benefits usually apply if:

- an employer/employee relationship exists, and
- the employee is injured in the furtherance of the employer's interests.

If a scholarship athlete is injured during either practice or a game, it would not be difficult to argue that the second requirement for workers' compensation benefits had been met. However, the first requirement of employer/employee relationship would remain problematic.

We might argue, contrary to the university's and athlete's view of the relationship, that instead we should look to the character of the relationship as represented by the presence of some or all of the following:

- The scholarship exists only as long as the athlete competes effectively. The National Collegiate Athletic Association requirement that the scholarship must continue to the end of the term is not enough to convince the legislature that the scholarship is not based on the "work" of competing performed by the athlete.
- The university claims to receive significant revenue and/or positive public relations value from the athlete's efforts on behalf of the school.
- The athlete may have entered the university on an academic basis less rigorous than nonathlete peers.

Nevada has enacted statutory law which includes intercollegiate athletes in its workers' compensation program.[1] California and Hawaii, on the other hand, have both explicitly excluded intercollegiate athletes from their workers' compensation legislation. Prior to explicitly excluding athletes from workers' compensation however, California case law included at least one instance in which an athlete was found to be an employee within the meaning of the state's workers' compensation laws at the time.[2] Although the California case involved the presence of additional evidence of an employer/employee relationship such as no-show, off-season employment that may have helped meet the workers' compensation requirements, it makes interesting reading.

The case law of other states, most notably Indiana (also Florida and Colorado), has found in favor of the university when faced with similar facts. The most that can be said with assurance about workers' compensation and the scholarship athlete is that only a few states have faced the issue either through case law or statute,

[1] An interesting review of the issue of workers' compensation and the scholarship athlete is "Comment: College Athletes Should Be Entitled to Workers' Compensation for Sports-Related Injuries" found in law libraries as well as on the internet at various law sites. 28 *Akron Law Review* 611 (1995).

[2] *Van Horn v Industrial Accident Commission.* 33 Cal. Reporter 169 (1963).

and therefore, it may be an interesting discussion point when considering relationships defined by overlapping actions of the parties and the law.

Relationships Defined by the Law

Teachers and students and coaches and athletes also have legal relationships with each other, but the obligations flowing out of these relationships are not defined by the parties. Instead they are defined by case and statutory law.

Most of the law-defined obligations that teachers owe students and that coaches owe athletes are found in case law. Case law is made up of the ever-increasing and changing body of court opinions and decisions created as lawsuits are decided. Jurisdictional boundaries apply to case law, so a teacher's obligations to students may vary somewhat from state to state and from federal jurisdiction to federal jurisdiction.

In addition to case law, statutory law (specific, written obligations imposed by the local, state, or federal government) sometimes imposes obligations and defines relationships. For instance, the U.S. Constitution's 14th Amendment, among other amendments and statutes, defines the obligation to avoid gratuitous classification followed by unequal treatment arising out of a relationship between a member of the public and someone, known as a "state actor," acting on behalf of a governmental entity. (A more complete discussion of who or what is a state actor is found in Chapter 12.)

Nature of the Role Being Played by the Person Owing a Duty

Regardless of the way a legal relationship is formed, whether it is formed by the parties or by law, the nature of the relationship defines the duties involved. The salary level of a party has nothing to do with the duties owed. So a volunteer soccer coach owes the athletes the same duties as a paid soccer coach. If the duties a paid soccer coach owes the athletes include such things as adequate supervision, access to emergency medical care, use of proper progressions, and safe facilities, the volunteer soccer coach owes the athletes the same duties. The fact that one coach is paid and the other is not has no effect on the duties owed to the athlete.

Nature of the Role Being Played by the Person to Whom the Duty is Owed

There are many situations which alter the level of effort that needs to be exerted to protect from harm someone to whom we owe a duty. For instance, in some states the level of supervision owed to a person varies, depending on if the individual is playing the role of a student in class or is playing the role of a recreating member of the community shooting a few hoops on school property. This variance is in addition to the varying level of the standard of care required relating to such things as the age and skill level of the participant and the hazardousness of the activity engaged in.

In some states, the effort a landowner needs to exert in order to protect a visitor from harm also varies with the nature of the person's presence. If the visitor is a trespasser, the effort required of the land-owner may be small. If the visitor is coming onto the owner's land for either the benefit of the landowner or the mutual benefit of the land owner and the visitor, then the visitor is classified as an invitee and is owed the effort of a prudent, reasonable, up-to-date land-owner in the protection from the foreseeable risk of unreasonable harm.

Some states make no distinction between the extremes of trespasser and invitee or student and recreator in relation to the level of care which must be exerted. However, because we often work in facilities to which visitors, recreators, and students come, either with an invitation or not, it is a good idea to find out what level of effort our particular state requires in varying circumstances. It is always the safest behavior to provide the standard of care equal to that which would be provided by the reasonable, prudent, up-to-date teacher, coach or administrator.

Memory Testers

1. True/False. The only duties which a teacher owes a student are the duties actually spelled out in the teacher's written contract.

2. True/False. A lifeguard who has agreed to work for the minimum wage has a lesser legal obligation (fewer legal duties) than a well-paid lifeguard.

3. True/False. A volunteer coach, because of the volunteer status, will always have a smaller and less rigorous set of duties than a paid coach.

Memory Tester Discussion

1. False.   Although a contract might specify particular duties owed to a teacher's students, the absence of those duties in the written contract does not indicate an absence of duties owed. Case law may call for the prudent teacher to use a high degree of supervision when teaching beginning swimming, yet no reference to swimming needs to be included in the contract or statutory law to impose such a duty. So a teacher's duties are in effect defined by case law and statutory law, and sometimes defined by the parties' specific contractual clauses.

2. False.   As ludicrous as this question seems, some employees think they owe their employer a less complete performance on the job just because they are not getting paid what they would like to be paid. They are wrong. Once someone takes on a role as a teacher, coach, lifeguard, and such, a set of duties is automatically required as part of that relationship.
Those duties have nothing to do with the amount of pay but rather depend solely on the existence of the relationship of teacher to student, coach to athlete, or lifeguard to swimmer.

3. False.   Duties relate to the role, not to the salary.

How Good Do I Have to Be?

Whether relationships and the concomitant obligations imposed on those within the relationship are defined by the parties or by law, there must be a method to determine if the parties to the relationship have been sufficiently diligent in meeting their respective obligations.

Material versus Nonmaterial Failure to Meet an Obligation

In contractually defined relationships, the general standard of sufficient performance is the threshold between a material breach of contract and an immaterial breach of contract. In other words, it's not so much an issue of how completely one party breached an obligation, but rather how important the obligation that was breached was to the basis of the contract.

For instance, if a coach has an obligation to hold a 3-hour practice and only holds a 2-hour, 45-minute practice, the coach has breached an obligation defined by the parties. Even though such behavior might be considered unprofessional, would such a breach be of sufficient importance (materiality) to be actionable? Let's compare the 15-minute breach during practice to a breach of the same length during a competitive event. In each case, the coach would be absent for 15 minutes, but one absence is arguably significantly more material than the other.

Imposition of Professional Standards

Relationships vary. You might be an experienced, highly-paid teacher relating to a class of beginners. You might be a volunteer with little skill beyond enthusiasm relating to a team of active 12 year olds participating in a high-risk activity. Do the vagaries of the status of the defendant have an impact on how closely the teacher or coach needs to adhere to professional standards?

People who hold themselves out to be coaches have the obligation to fulfill the accepted professional standards of coaches. The same applies to people who hold themselves out to be teachers.

The obligation to meet professional standards applies whether the coach or teacher is a professional in the sense of being paid or the person is a volunteer. The trigger to the obligation to meet professional standards is the role played by the person rather than the person's payroll status.

The need to professionally meet the obligations imposed by a relationship does not vary between paid and unpaid individuals. This statement has a great deal of significance for those who volunteer their services as coaches, officials, and organizers of youth sports programs. Many personnel in youth sports programs are volunteers. In addition, these volunteers often assume (erroneously) that because they are volunteers, they don't have to be as good at what they are doing as paid coaches, officials, or organizers. This misconception can be of great significance to volunteer and participant alike, because the volunteer might not set standards as high as they need to be, and thereby the participant could be provided with less than professional leadership. If the volunteer's failure to meet the professional standard results in an injury to a participant, it is possible that the volunteer could face claims of negligence.

Standards exist for the manufacture of some items of sporting equipment. Standards of behavior are sometimes set forth in employee manuals. Safety standards have been adopted for the conduct of swimming classes. Whenever the profession has promulgated standards, those standards set a rebuttable presumption of what the minimum level of obligatory performance should be.

Let's assume that accepted professional standards say that three lifeguards should be on duty for a swimming program of X number of people in a pool of Y size. If the pool supervisor who carries out the obligation to provide lifeguards does so at a level below the accepted professional standard, that supervisor is presumed not to have been "good enough." The presumption might be rebutted if evidence demonstrated that the level of safety and supervision at the pool was not diminished by the lower standard; however, proving a negative is always difficult. The wise professional (paid or unpaid) makes certain to meet existing professional standards of conduct.

Policy/Standards Manuals

Program administrators often develop policy manuals to set standards of practice for their programs. For instance, the manual might include standards or policies to be followed concerning supervision, schedule for safety checks of facilities, frequency of rehabilitating and/or replacing equipment, contraindicated exercise, and emergency procedures in case of injury.

The existence of policy manuals helps those in the program know what is expected of them—how good they have to be. However, often policy manuals are in the files gathering dust, and employees within the program don't know what the policies are.

If an employee who is accused of negligence has failed to follow a policy of the employer, it is possible that questions may arise about whether the employee met the standard of care, or in other words, that the employee's behavior may not have been good enough. The employee can then try to show that the level of behavior was good enough even if it didn't match the behavior specified in the policy manual, but that is often difficult to do. So it is a good idea to have policy manuals in existence, and it is a good idea to have employees aware of their contents.

First, the policies, if well designed, help the employee know what level of performance is deemed by the program administrators or professional association to be prudent, reasonable, and up-to-date, and if followed by the employee, injuries might be averted. Second, the presence of policies helps the employer demonstrate that the program is conducted in a prudent, reasonable, and up-to-date manner by specifying to the program's employees the level of performance expected.

Legal Relationships and Obligations

Relationships must exist before legal obligations are owed.

Relationships can be created either by the parties involved or by the action of law.

Relationships created by the action of law may be created either by case law or by statutory law.

Failure to meet professional standards creates a rebuttable presumption of failure to meet required standard of care.

Practice Scenario

Practice your understanding of the concepts we've been talking about by evaluating this scenario:

Jan, a volunteer coach for a Saturday youth sport community soccer team, works hard at teaching the team soccer skills, practicing various competitive strategies, conditioning the players through a variety of exercises, and building a sense of teamwork and personal worth through team activities. Jan has no formal training in coaching techniques but believes playing experience, enthusiasm, and hard work can make up for a lack of formal training as a coach.

When Jan was a player, Jan's coach withheld water from the players in an effort to make them focus on the game rather than personal comfort and individual desires. A warm-up sequence involving straight-legged sit-ups, leg lifts, hurdler's exercises, and various exercises using bicycling motions while the body's weight is borne on the neck also characterized Jan's playing experience. Jan incorporates both the water restriction and warm-up sequence into the coaching routine.

- *Consider Jan's duties as a volunteer coach: Do they differ from a paid coach?*
- *Consider the impact of Jan's lack of formal training in relationship to Jan's performance as a coach: Does Jan's lack of training automati-*

*cally mean Jan has breached a duty, or is it Jan's actual perfor-
mance which matters?*

- *What presumptions regarding professional standards might be made
  by the courts concerning Jan's coaching methods if a team member
  were injured either by the water restriction or warm-up routine?*

Standard of Care

Standard of care is a concept of legal significance in negligence
cases. One of the four required elements for negligence cases is *duty*.
In other words, a defendant cannot be successfully sued if there is
no obligation or duty owed by the defendant to the plaintiff.

In negligence cases, the existence of the duty or obligation arises
out of case law rather than by a negotiation process between the
parties. The duty owed is formed from the relationship that exists,
such as the teacher/student relationship or the coach/athlete relationship.

The standard of care, or how good the teacher's professional
performance has to be in meeting the duty owed to the student,
depends on a great many factors. However, one factor it does *not*
depend on is the experience or ability of the individual teacher (except in the case of a teacher claiming some special expertise or certification beyond the norm). Once someone is in the role of a teacher,
that person must live up to the standard of care of a reasonable,
prudent, up-to-date teacher, even if in actuality the teacher (or coach)
is unreasonable, imprudent, or out-of-date.

So the more experience and ability a teacher possesses, the better for all concerned. The standard of care sets a minimum level at
which a legal obligation may be met. The standard is not lowered
because the person performing the obligation is less skilled. Nor is
the minimum standard for performance raised simply because a
teacher is better than the minimum. A better teacher doesn't carry
greater responsibilities or obligations in a legal sense. A better teacher,
without being legally obligated to do so, simply does a better job
and carries out the duties owed better.

Simply stated, **the duty owed is to protect the student or athlete from the foreseeable risk of unreasonable harm.** Although it
may be stated simply, the duty is not a simple duty. The responsibility placed on the teacher or coach to meet the obligation varies
according to circumstance.

For instance, it may vary because of:

- age or maturity of participants,
- skill of participants
- health and conditioning status of the participants
- size of class/team
- complexity of activity
- hazardous nature of the activity
- age, skill, size of the competitors/participants
- amount of supervision present
- significance of safety hazards present due to facilities or equipment
- atmosphere/logistics/nature of the area in which the activity will take place (visibility, traffic, time of day, criminal element)
- accessibility of medical assistance.

Let's discuss a few of these variables. When participants are youthful or less prepared to protect themselves for other reasons, such as developmental or behavioral problems, the teacher's minimum obligation for supervision increases. There may therefore be a need to have more supervisors or fewer students, or whatever supervisors are present must exhibit more intense supervision.

Much has been written on the use of general versus specific supervision. The selection of the type of supervision is closely related to the standard of care. Obviously, as a class gets bigger, it will require more supervision. As the nature of the students or activity changes, the need for more specific versus general supervision may change.

The degree of danger in the activity is also a basis for altering the standard of care owed. High-risk activities such as swimming and gymnastics generally require a higher standard of care than a basketball class. In a swimming class, a lifeguard should always be present even if the swimmers are adults or excellent swimmers. Some levels of supervision are determined by factors other than the size of the class or the age of the students; the standard of care is determined by the potential for serious injury existing in either the nature of the equipment (fencing or riflery) or the location (busy streets).

The health and conditioning level of the participants also have an impact on the standard of care to which the teacher is obligated.

Legal Relationships and Obligations

Legal obligations arise out of relationships. Relationships can be defined by the parties or by the action of law.

Once a legal obligation exists, a standard of performance is imposed that sets the minimum acceptable level of performance. The standard might be set by the parties in a contractual arrangement or by statute or by the cumulative wisdom of case law.

The standard of care required may vary, particularly in negligence settings, by the presence or absence of a number of factors, such as the skill, age, and maturity of the participants, the nature of the activity, and the degree of risk involved.

Therefore, it is important for the teacher to know issues of a health-related nature that affect the student's participation; a teacher cannot meet an obligation in ignorance. The teacher must plan a progressive conditioning program so the participants are appropriately conditioned and so the teacher knows the conditioning level of each student. Goals of the activity may need to be set differently if health or conditioning levels are less than favorable.

A student with a heart problem or recent stress fracture or one who has been out of activity for an extended period of time is owed a greater standard of care than a well-conditioned, healthy student. If the activity is performed in an excessively hot environment, or if no swift access to medical care is possible, a much greater standard of care needs to be shown. That standard of care may exhibit itself by excluding a student from participation, finding alternative activities, arranging for a car and driver to be available when the activity takes place at a remote location so any injured student has quick access to medical care, and so forth.

Memory Testers

1. True/False. A volunteer does not have to meet the same standard of care required of a paid teacher.
2. True/False. The duties and obligations involved in a negligence setting arise most frequently out of relationships defined by the parties rather than by the law.

3. True/False. A teacher's experience does not alter the standard of care required.

4. True/False. In most jurisdictions, someone who happened to be passing by a lakeshore and noticed a swimmer in trouble would have no legal obligation to try to help.

5. True/False. The standard of care applied to teachers is, "What would the reasonable person do in the same circumstances?"

Memory Tester Discussion

1. False. Standard of care is defined by the role rather than by the issue of being paid or unpaid. As soon as a person adopts the role of being a teacher or coach, that person is held to the legal standard of care required of the role of teacher or coach.

2. False. The definition of the relationships involved in negligence situations arises most frequently out of case law. The teachers and students do not typically sit down and negotiate their respective legal obligations.

3. True. Once people hold themselves out to be teachers, they subject themselves to the minimum level of performance requirements (standard of care) that go along with the role. Additional years of experience will make them a better teacher but will not alter the standard of care required.

4. True. Although there might be a moral obligation to seek assistance/help, there is generally no legal obligation. This is so because there is no relationship between the passerby and the troubled swimmer. A swimmer in a swimming class would, on the other hand, be owed a full set of obligations by the lifeguard and instructor because a relationship exists.

Even though there may not exist any obligation to save a drowning stranger, there are obligations between strangers in other circumstances. For instance, let's assume you were enjoying a sight-seeing trip to the top of the Empire State Building, and you decided to test out some of Galileo's findings by throwing a brick over the edge. If a pedestrian below was hit by the brick, one of the kindest things that could be said about you is that your actions as a brick thrower were negligent. Did you know the brick's recipient? No, there was no relationship between you and the pedestrian, but you owed the pedestrian, as well as the rest of the members of society, a duty anyway. As members of society, we all have the obligation to act in such a way that our carelessness doesn't result in significant harm to another.

5. False. A teacher's performance is not judged by what a reasonable person would do. A teacher is expected to have a higher degree of skill and ability to foresee risk than an ordinary person. Therefore, the correct standard for a teacher would be to do what "a prudent, reasonable, up-to-date *teacher* in the same circumstances" would do.

How About Looking Up a Few Cases?

You might find it interesting to read some of the following cases. Some have value as precedents within their jurisdictions; others don't. Don't assume that the outcome would be the outcome in your jurisdiction. However, read them to gain an insight into how the issues are evaluated. As you read them, develop arguments of your own for the plaintiff and then for the defendant.

Rensing v. Indiana State University, 437 N.E. 2d 78 (Inc. App. 1982) rev'd 444 N.E. 2d 1170 (Inc. 1983). This is a workers' compensation case involving a catastrophically injured football player.

Van Horn v. Industrial Accident Commission, 219 Cal. App. 2d 457, 33 Cal. Rptr. 169 (1963). Although the case is older, the facts in this workers' compensation case involving a college scholarship athlete killed in a plane crash returning from a game make interesting reading and provide a perspective on the issue of scholarship athletes and workers' compensation.

Tanari v. School Directors, 373 N.E. 2d 5 (1977). Who is an invitee or a licensee or a trespasser? This case involves a visitor to a high school football game who is injured. What is the standard of care to which the visitor holding a complimentary pass is entitled?

Chapter 5

Negligence: "Oops!"

In the legal sense, a tort is a civil rather than criminal wrong. Some examples of torts are negligence, defamation, civil battery, malicious interference with a contractual right, and false imprisonment. Negligence differs from the other torts because negligence is unintentional.

When a child who spilled milk cries, "I didn't mean to!" the child is not denying negligence. Why does the child utter such a cry if it does not absolve one of negligence? Perhaps the child utters its cry because society looks more harshly at someone who intends to hurt or damage another, even though the hurt or damage is identical to that caused unintentionally by someone else. That same differentiation applies at least to the categorization of torts, if not to the penalties imposed.

Negligence—The Unintentional Tort

Action versus Inaction

Negligence can result either from action or inaction. Carelessness can result in injury. Carelessness can take the form of poorly thought-out actions (errors of commission), or carelessness can take the form of refraining from acting when action should be taken (error of omission). Whether by commission or omission, carelessness can be the basis for claims of negligence. For instance, the carelessness of a teacher who places a relay race's finish line within a few feet of the gymnasium wall might result in an injury due to the teacher's act of commission. A teacher who, in the midst of a class activity, ignores the distress of a student with heart problems might be negligent and thus responsible for damage to the student's heart caused by the activity via the notion of an act of omission (failure to act).

The Four Required Elements of Negligence

Before a teacher would have to assume financial responsibility for a student's injury, the teacher would have to be found guilty of negligence. In order to be found guilty of negligence, four elements need to exist: duty, breach, cause, and harm.

Duty

Duty is defined either by the parties or by law (legal obligations and relationships are more fully discussed in Chapter 4). Over the centuries, legal scholars have tried to identify the triggering mechanism giving rise to a legal duty but have never been wholly successful in the attempt. The best attempt yielded so far is, "Courts will find a duty where, in general, reasonable persons would recognize it and agree that it exists."

A universal determination of when a duty arises is yet to be crafted, but we do know that there is a legal relationship, and thus a duty, between teachers and their students and between coaches and their athletes. The duty owed between teachers and students, coaches and athletes, can be stated as "the duty to protect from the foreseeable risk of unreasonable harm." In more specific terms, the duty might find expression in such subduties as:

- providing proper instruction,
- providing a level of supervision appropriate for the activity's risk and the age, skill, and understanding of participants,

---

[1] W. P. Keeton. (1984). *Prosser and Keeton on Torts* (5th ed., p.359). St. Paul, MN: West Publishing.

- using safe progressions,
- providing access to medical help in case of injury,
- using safe facilities and equipment, or
- teaching appropriate safety procedures.

Breach

Once the existence of a duty has been established, the plaintiff will need to show that the duty was breached. Breach is the failure to meet one's duties or obligations. If a teacher fails to use proper teaching techniques, the teacher will have breached a duty. A swimming teacher who allows students to dive in shallow water has breached a duty. A coach who leaves the field while practice continues has breached a duty. A department chair who knows that facilities are hazardous and yet allows classes to continue in the facilities has breached a duty to provide safe facilities.

The issue of standard of care (see Chapter 4 for a fuller discussion of this issue) is part of the consideration of the element "breach." Standard of care is a term of art (special meaning), which defines how diligent someone needs to be in order to avoid breaching a duty so significantly as to have that breach considered as meeting the required element of breach in a negligence case.

Not every breach of a duty yields negligence. The remaining two elements must also be present. For example, if your school's principal requires you to file a lesson plan for each day's teaching effort and you fail to do so, you have breached a duty, but if no one is injured thereby, you are not negligent. If your student's hands slip off the bars during a gymnastics unit because you neither provided chalk nor taught the safety impact of using chalk, are you then guilty of negligence because of the missing lesson plan? No, your failure to file a lesson plan was a breach, but it was not the one that caused the injury; the breach of the missing lesson plan was unrelated to the cause of the student's injury. However, the breach concerning the chalk was a breach that might have caused the injury and thus might subject you to claims of negligence. The difference in result from the two breaches (lesson plan and chalk) is because the third required element of negligence, "cause," must exist.

Cause

Cause, as a required element of all negligence claims, is the subject of extended legal discussion. Almost any action or lack of action can be said to have contributed to an injurious result, but when does that contribution rise to a level sufficient to support a claim of negligence?

At the end of legal discussions about the meanings of "proximate cause," "cause in fact," and "legal cause," we probably would arrive at the same conclusion concerning the meaning of "cause" that most people do just by using common sense. The contribution made to the cause of an injury by a particular breach must rise to the level society requires to establish fault (see Chapter 3 for a fuller discussion of blame and fault).

To teachers, coaches, and administrators, the notion of "cause" as an element of negligence has great significance even if legal scholars continue to debate its exact meaning. As teachers, coaches, and administrators, we know it is difficult to pass through our professional lives without breaching a duty now and then. For most of us, fortunately, those breaches do not cause an injury, but we learn from these close encounters with negligence and then conduct our professional lives differently in the future. Only a stupid teacher, coach, or administrator would wait for a particular practice to injure someone before acknowledging that the action or inaction breaches a duty.

Smart teachers, coaches, and administrators learn from experience, even if no injury is involved. Experience is a valued commodity which allows us to change before injuries occur.

Harm

Harm is the fourth element required for negligence. Absence of harm means there is no negligence. The old basketball phrase applies: "No harm, no foul."

Technically, any physical injury fulfills the element of "harm." However, the trier of fact (jury) determines if an injury is sufficient to demonstrate that the teacher breached the duty to protect students from the foreseeable risk of unreasonable harm. A mild bruise in a game of basketball is not an unreasonable harm. A broken ankle may be. The jury draws the line between reasonable and unreasonable harm.

Emotional or psychological harm is treated differently from physical harm by the courts. Some jurisdictions will allow recovery for emotional or psychological harm, but of those which do, most require that physical harm must also be claimed. In other words, in those jurisdictions allowing recovery for emotional or psychological harm, most require the presence of physical injury before even considering emotional or psychological injury.

Four Required Elements of Negligence

1. Duty
2. Breach
3. Cause
4. Harm

CHALLENGE REVIEW

Elements of Negligence

Consider the fact patterns below, which have in most cases been adapted from real lawsuits, and decide which of the four required elements of negligence is the issue in each. Resist the temptation to try to decide who won the case. Instead, focus on which of the four elements is the issue.

1. During a written quiz on safety rules, the teacher left the room. As one of the young students was about to sit down, another student held a pencil vertically beneath the sitting student, causing severe injuries.

2. A student died after accidentally being hit in the head with a golf club during an indoor physical education class. The arrangement of mats varied from that suggested by the school district's formal curriculum. The student was not familiar with the game of golf and had not attended the first class in which instruction and practice were provided, nor had the student received any instruction from the teacher but only from the fellow student who struck the fatal blow.

3. A young student was injured on the monkey bars when the student swung to a pole and, while sliding down it, cut a leg on a screw protruding from the pole. There were about 150 to 180 elementary school children under the supervision of one teacher.

4. A student fell during a running activity on the track. The teacher had no written lesson plan for the day.

5. One of two students using neighboring treadmills at the school's fitness room told a joke to a friend standing nearby. When the punch line of the joke arrived, the eavesdropping student on the second treadmill found it so funny that it caused the student to lose concentration, misstep, and fall off the moving treadmill. A fitness center supervisor was in the room providing general supervision. The injured student sued, among others, the teller of the joke.

Challenge Review Hints

1. Could the teacher have prevented the injury if he or she had been present and supervised appropriately? (Cause.)

2. Did the unconventional placement of the mats cause the injury? (Cause.) Would a prudent, up-to-date teacher have reviewed the material presented in the lesson the previously absent student had missed? (Breach.) Whose duty is it to inspect the equipment, and how often should the equipment be inspected? (Duty.)

3. How often should the equipment be inspected? (Breach.) Would frequent inspection have barred the injury? (Cause.) Would an increased amount of supervision have made a difference? (Cause.)

4. Was the student injured? (Harm.) In spite of the lack of a lesson plan, was the lesson conducted appropriately? (Breach.)

5. Did the person on the adjacent treadmill owe the co-exerciser a duty to avoid telling funny jokes within earshot of any person on a treadmill? (Duty.) Did the joke telling cause the injury? (Cause.) If the joke had not been funny, should the legal result have been different? (Breach? Standard of care?)

Memory Testers: Elements of Negligence

1. True/False. If you follow professional guidelines and someone is injured, you cannot be successfully sued for negligence.

2. True/False. If you owed a duty to a student and you breached that duty, you were negligent.

3. True/False. In jurisdictions in which the notion of joint and several liability is applied, if two coaches are found liable by the court for negligent behavior and the court awards the injured athlete $100,000, the athlete will only collect $50,000 maximum if one of the coaches has no money.

4. True/False. Negligence is, by definition, unintentional.

5. True/False. An administrator who fails to check the references of a new employee may be found guilty of negligence if the employee's lack of training (which would have been apparent had the references been checked) causes an injury to a student.

Memory Tester Discussion

1. False. Following professional guidelines provides a rebuttable presumption that your behavior at least meets the standard of care that would be met by a prudent, up-to-date teacher, coach, or administrator in the same circumstances. This is comforting, but it is not a total security blanket. The presumption is rebuttable. That means that the plaintiff can try to demonstrate either that the guidelines are defective or that to follow them in the particular circumstances of the case was inappropriate.

2. False. You cannot be negligent in a legal sense unless your breach caused an injury.

3. False. Joint and several liability means that each defendant is liable individually for the total $100,000. If one of the defendants cannot pay, the other will have to carry the full burden. Of course, the plaintiff cannot collect more than the total amount awarded, so even if both defendants have lots of money, the plaintiff can only receive a total of $100,000, regardless of who pays what portion.

4. True. Negligence is an unintentional tort.

5. True. An administrator owes a duty to students, athletes, and others to hire prudent, up-to-date staff members.

If the administrator breaches that duty and a participant in the program is harmed thereby, the administrator may be successfully sued for negligence.

Can You Be Negligent Even If You Are Not Actively Involved?

Yes. You can be found guilty of negligence even if you are not the individual who either acted or failed to act in a negligent manner. The legal theory of agency allows the placement of liability for negligence on the principal (authority giver) for whom the agent acted. The doctrine of *respondeat superior* allows the placement of liability for negligent acts of an employee on the shoulders of the employer.

Agency

If, as a teacher, you direct a student leader to carry out a responsibility in a particular way, which turns out to cause injury to another student, and the method you had the student leader use would fail the standard of care test (what a prudent, up-to-date, reasonable teacher would do in similar circumstances), you, as the teacher, might be successfully sued for negligence. The student leader might be considered your agent.

The liability for the acts of an agent in the service of the principal is, in most instances, attributable to the principal. The ability to sue the principal is helpful to the injured plaintiff because it is more likely that the principal has more money to pay a judgment than the agent. Those who direct the actions of another should be aware that they face potential liability. When teachers or administrators ask others to act as their agents, they should be careful to describe how they want their agents to act in order to avoid injuring anyone and, thereby, avoid claims of negligence.

Respondeat Superior

The doctrine of *respondeat superior* says that the superior (employer) is responsible for the negligence of the superior's employees. It must be added swiftly, however, that the doctrine of *respondeat superior* does not relieve the employee of responsibility. Instead, it provides the plaintiff with a second place to look for recovery for the results of negligent acts. Similar to the notion that the principal in a principal/agent relationship is likely to be better able to pay a judgment, it is assumed that the employer is better able to pay a judgment than the employee.

So if you are the boss or even a middle-level boss, you need to be aware that you may be held liable whenever an employee is found negligent in the course of the employee's job-related duties. This knowledge should encourage you to pay attention to the following items in relation to those who work in your program, including volunteers:

- careful and thorough preemployment review of resumes, recommendations, and qualifications,
- preservice training,
- supervision,
- development and adherence to appropriate curricula and procedures,
- inservice instruction,
- attendance at conferences and conventions so that your staff stays up-to-date,
- open-minded evaluation of complaints from students, athletes, and parents so that problems that could lead to claims of negligence are avoided before an injury occurs, and
- open-minded evaluation of incidents and accidents so that changes in procedures and curricula can be made where appropriate.

Can Your Words Make You Negligent?

Yes, you can be found negligent, assuming all the other elements of negligence are present, if your words or actions induce reliance. For instance, consider the following situation: A school says that a security guard is always on duty at the entrance to the parking lot in the evenings, but one evening the guard is not present. A new teacher, in reliance on the expected presence of the guard, enters the parking lot alone, is attacked by someone whom the guard, if present, would have kept from entering the parking lot. Even though the school originally may not have had a duty to provide a guard, its words stating a guard would be present made the new teacher more vulnerable to injury than if the school had said nothing about the guard. Thus the school has assumed a duty by its words.

---

[2] Restatement (Second) of Torts, sections 311 and 552.

A second theory, in addition to the *assumed duty* theory, upon which a plaintiff might base a negligence claim based on words alone, would be *negligent misrepresentation*. Let's consider an example. You are an Olympic gymnast visiting a school for a day. When a student justifiably relies on your apparently thought-out advice that the student is ready to attempt a new, challenging gymnastic skill yet your advice was not thought out, a duty may be breached by you. As a visitor to the school, you do not owe a particular duty to the student. But you assume a duty once you undertake to advise the student and the student reasonably relies on your advice regarding the gymnastics movement.

Not every carelessly uttered statement would give rise to a claim of negligence, however. First, a duty to exercise reasonable care in giving the information must exist. That duty arises when it is foreseeable that the hearer of the statement would rely on the information contained in the statement, that it would be reasonable to expect the speaker to know that the information is desired by the hearer for a serious purpose and, if relied on, might cause injury.

Sometimes, like people in other professions, we let our egos get the best of us and offer advice to others either without having the specific expertise to make valid recommendations or without spending the time to correctly understand the underlying situations which might make our advice inadvisable. Bad advice can produce bad results. Bad results can produce claims of negligence. The best advice is for us to take our profession seriously and take our words seriously.

Can You Be Negligent for the Acts of Unrelated Third Parties?

Yes, you can be negligent, if the injured party is someone to whom you owed a duty. Acts of violence in school settings are an increasingly frequent occurrence. Consider a scenario in which a third party (a student from another class, another school, or even someone totally unconnected with the school) enters the school and attacks one of your students.

If the administration has not met its duty to act prudently in its attempts to maintain a safe campus, the administration might be found guilty of negligence. If a teacher sends a young student to the office without escort and is deemed not to have acted prudently in doing so because of accessibility of the campus to unsupervised individuals, the teacher might be found guilty of negligence. If a coach knows that a particular athlete has a bad temper and has a propensity for violence yet allows the athlete to play when angry, a victim of the athlete's violent act, even if from an opposing school, might be able to successfully sue the coach for negligence.

In each of the scenarios above, the administration, teacher, and coach had a duty to the injured student. Sometimes that duty extends to those not normally under supervision, such as in the case of the coach's duty to protect the visiting athlete from the foreseeable risk of unreasonable harm.

In each instance, the potential for harm was foreseeable. Prudent precautions such as stricter control over who comes on campus, escorting young students in hallways, or barring athletes with demonstrated violent propensities from situations in which they have become angered were not taken. Therefore, a duty was breached. If the breach resulted in injury, negligence existed.

How Do You Avoid Being Negligent?

The answer to this question is simple: Be an up-to-date, prudent teacher, coach, or administrator and be certain that those who work for you are also up-to-date, prudent teachers, coaches, or administrators.

Practice Scenario

1. An athletic trainer tells an injured athlete that it is safe to return to competition but does so without really knowing so.

   • Has the athletic trainer breached a duty to the athlete?
   • Explain the legal issues involved.

2. An after-school track practice is held on the school's field. Access to all school phones ends when the offices are locked at 3:00 PM. A student member of the track team is injured, and medical help is delayed because of the lack of access to a phone.

   • Would the prudent coach and administrator have developed policies for providing access to a telephone on the field?

- Would it matter if the delay did not exacerbate the injury?
- Would a duty have been breached even if the initial cause of the injury had nothing to do with negligence?

3. A student is injured during a beginning, 7th-grade fencing class when the teacher steps out of the room to talk to another teacher in the hall.

    - Does it matter if the injury would have occurred even if the teacher had been present?
    - Is the teacher relieved of all duties owed to the students once the teacher leaves the room, even in the middle of class?
    - What element(s) of negligence is/are the issue?
    - Would the issues be any different if the class had been a modern dance class composed of expert dancers in the 12th grade?

4. The facilities are in a bad state of repair at Urban High School due to severe budget cuts and years of deferred maintenance. One day during a physical education class, a lighting fixture falls from the ceiling and narrowly misses two students.

    - What duties have been breached?
    - Are all the elements of negligence present?

How About Looking Up Some Cases?

You might find it interesting to read some of the following cases. Some have value as precedents within their jurisdiction, others do not. Don't assume that the outcome would be the outcome in your jurisdiction. Read them to gain an insight into how the issues of negligence are evaluated. Try to develop arguments of your own for the plaintiff and then for the defendant. If you are using the internet to find these cases, take a look at the Appendix for a few suggested cites to check.

> *Brahatcek v Millard School District*, 273 NW 2d 680 (1979). This older case brings up a current problem: What duty to update do we owe to a student who has been absent?

Darrow v. West Genesee Central School District, 41 AD 2d 897 (1973). This reasonably old case presents interesting legal issues about a teacher's duty to provide safety instructions and, indeed, the appropriateness of specific activities such as line soccer.

Halper v. Vayo, 568 N.E. Rptr 2d, 914 (1991). A high school wrestling coach attempted to treat a wrestler's knee injury. The central issue was potential immunity, but the discussion of the coach's duty to obtain medical care and monitor the return to participation following injury provides for interesting discussion points.

Heard v. The City of New York, 82 NY2d 66, 623 N.E. 2d 541, 603 NYS2d 414 (1993) This case involves a beach lifeguard's giving in to a swimmer's request for "one more" dive in shallow water from a jetty. The dive resulted in a paralyzing injury, and the case revolves around the negligence not of actions but of the words of the lifeguard.

Mogabgab v. Orleans Parish School Board, 239 So. 2d 456 (1970). This old but fascinating case revolves around coaches who ordered full-uniform football practices in Louisiana in the summertime while denying fluid replacement to their athletes. When a student became ill and was denied medical care, the issue became "cause."

Chapter 6

Defusing Negligence Liability

Earlier in this book we discussed the concept of legal fault (blame) and legal obligation (liability). This chapter is devoted to the concept of managing the potential imposition of legal fault and/or unwanted legal obligation in the context of negligence claims.

Risk management, a term found in many conversations these days, is more than the employment of available defenses. At its best, risk management in relation to negligence is an integrated strategy for both conducting safe programs and reducing the potential for loss arising from successful legal claims against the program, its individual employees, and administrators.

Risk management strategy involves several steps, including:

- identification of risks,
- evaluation of risks, and
- management of risks.

Identification of Risks

It is impossible to be proactive if risks are not known. A dangerous procedure cannot be altered, an increased supervision level will not be instituted, if no potential for danger is perceived. Therefore, potential risks must be identified before the risk becomes an incident or accident. A few places to begin looking for risks are: facilities and equipment, staffing, participant population, policies and procedures, and program offerings.

Facilities and Equipment

Homemade or out-of-date equipment, areas of deferred maintenance, structural designs of gymnasiums that don't match today's sports, security from unauthorized entry, and security of equipment when not in use are all worthy of close and continuing review.

Inspections of facilities and equipment should be conducted on a scheduled basis and the results documented. Any unsafe condition should be corrected swiftly, and if not immediately correctable, the facilities or equipment should be removed from use until repaired or replaced.

Budget constraints often result in administrators having to make difficult choices between maintaining safety or continuing to run programs at all. Pragmatism should not be allowed to cause an administrator to turn away from the realities of legal duty. The coach or teacher who is frustrated by having repair requests ignored by administrators should not turn away from his or her own legal duty to participants. There is no way out of owing the duty of providing safe facilities and equipment to students and athletes, regardless of the realities of budget cuts.

Staffing

The use of uncertified teachers is not, all by itself, a breach of duty. Certification is not a safeguard against claims of negligence. Instead, the presence of proper certification simply makes it slightly easier for the supervisor who has been accused of hiring inept teachers or coaches to demonstrate that proper care had been taken in the hiring process. Certification brings with it an assumption (fully rebuttable, of course) that the teacher or coach had been suitably trained in prudent, nonnegligent techniques and perceptions. The teacher's or coach's actions, if negligent, will always speak louder than the presence of a certificate. On the other hand, the absence of certification does not guarantee that a teacher or coach will act in negligent ways.

Are coaches and teachers performing their duties up to standard? If observations are not periodically conducted, how can the administrator identify problems? Similarly, the administrator who refuses to investigate student or athlete complaints is omitting an important potential source of identification of risks.

Participant Population

Risks differ depending on such things as class size, age and conditioning level of participants, and presence of prerequisite skills among the participants. Some participants within a group are difficult to control; others listen closely and behave properly. These types of differences, as well as others, alter the level of risk. Coaches, administrators, and teachers need to identify the risks as they might exist in a particular participant population.

Policies and Procedures

Policies and procedures—from how to cope with medical emergencies to the frequency of equipment inspections—should be developed. The absence of appropriate policies and procedures usually means that the staff has not been thorough in its efforts to foresee risks.

Program Offerings

Sports and activities appropriate for some populations are not appropriate for others. The timing and placement of various activities also carry potential for increasing or decreasing risks. Supervision assignments should take into account the specific programming requirements. Assignment of teachers and coaches should also be responsive to the programmatic requirements for expertise, experience, and related qualifications.

Evaluation of Risks

After potential risks have been identified, they need to be evaluated. Which are life threatening, which are remediable, and which are likely to bring about injuries are questions for which answers need to be provided.

If liability were to be incurred for a particular risk, what would be the extent of the financial risk or risk to the reputation of the program? What options exist to decrease risks, and what is their cost in money, time, and administrative supervision? Without such knowledge, it is very difficult to weigh different options for managing risks.

Management of Risks

After risks are identified and evaluated, they must be managed. Risk management involves a decision-making process. Each identified and evaluated risk should be subjected to a series of questions. The answers to the questions will form the basis for determining the management technique selected to deal with the risk. For example:

- Is the particular risk acceptable?
- Is the risk so great that it cannot be tolerated (either injury or cost)?
- Is there an appropriate and efficacious means of reducing and removing the risk?
- Can we budget for the cost of paying for losses associated with liability?

If a risk cannot be removed totally, it must be (1) reduced as much as possible and then accepted, or (2) reduced as much as possible and the potential liability transferred.

Removing or Reducing Risks

To use an obvious example, a tour of your facilities identifies that your swimming pool lacks a door and thus there is a substantial risk of unauthorized individuals using the pool. Your evaluation of the risk determines that the risk is extremely serious since anyone could enter the pool, swim without supervision, and potentially drown. You have the following options:

- Remove or reduce the risk by repairing and replacing the door, installing a substantial lock, set and follow policies concerning the possession and access to the key, post clear and obvious notices banning use of the pool without authorization and lifeguards, and accept the reduced risk of a later, unauthorized entry in violation of your policies.

- Accept the risk and do nothing about the door. Your liability for the drowning or other pool injury would be unabated.
- Do nothing and transfer as much of the risk as possible (hoping that your inaction does not rise to the level of gross negligence, which would negate any effort to transfer liability and leave you totally liable).

Transferring Liability

The techniques used to reduce the risks are the same techniques any professional teacher, coach, or administrator would know and should use. The techniques used to transfer the risks might be less familiar to the prudent, up-to-date professional, thus we'll review them here.

Management of Risks
Remove
Reduce
Transfer

Liability can be transferred to others on the basis of contractual obligations, such as through the purchase of insurance; hold harmless laws, which exist as a product of the contractual employment relationship between public school teachers and their employers; through waivers, which are contractual relationships between you or your program and your adult participants; or through the statutory action of immunity and Good Samaritan laws.

Liability can also be transferred to the plaintiff in a non contractual way if the plaintiff breached the duty to self (contributory or comparative negligence) or if the plaintiff accepts the risks (assumption of risk).

Insurance

Professional liability insurance is available from a number of organizations in which professionals in the various fields of athletics, health, physical education, recreation, and dance would logically be members.

Professional liability insurance from any source generally protects the insured from expenses incurred in the defense of a lawsuit and, if the insured loses the lawsuit, will pay any judgments against the insured to the extent of the policy limits. Any judgment in excess of the policy limits would have to be paid by the insured.

It is wise to have professional liability insurance even if you are protected by other liability-shifting mechanisms such as hold harmless laws. The insurance may not cover anything additional, but when you are faced with a lawsuit, it is comforting to have as many people on your side as you can, and the low cost of professional liability insurance is an easy and inexpensive way to add to your feelings of being supported.

Umbrella policies that you might have in addition to either your car or home insurance are not the same as professional liability insurance policies. Indeed, most umbrella policies will *not* cover any of your professional activities at all. So read your umbrella policies (if you have them) and think about obtaining professional liability insurance as well.

Professional liability insurance does not protect against intentional torts or gross negligence. Instead it protects only against a claim of ordinary negligence that occurs in the furtherance of your professional activities. This is important to keep in mind because when you write a peer review report, you won't be protected if the report is later found to be an act of defamation. Neither will you be protected for claims based on sexual harassment, discrimination, or carelessness that rise to the extent of being considered gross negligence. (Gross negligence does not refer to the grossness of the injury but rather to the degree of carelessness causing the injury.)

Ultra Vires Activities

Professional liability insurance[1] will only protect you from claims of ordinary negligence occurring in the furtherance of your professional duties. If you organize a Saturday car wash to raise money for your team and someone at the car wash is hurt because of your negligence, it is possible that professional liability insurance would not defend you because organizing a car wash was not part of your duties.

Activities outside your job duties are called *ultra vires* activities. We all get ourselves into *ultra vires* situations (such as the car wash above), but we need to realize that we may also be putting ourselves in positions of great exposure to potential liability.

---

[1] The American Alliance for Health, Physical Education, Recreation and Dance makes professional liablity insurance available to members. Contact AAHPERD at 1900 Association Drive, Reston, VA 22091, (703) 476-3400.

Another example of an activity that might be *ultra vires* occurs when we transport students. When we transport students in our personal cars, our personal insurance generally is not affected and in case of injury, recovery to the policy limits is available. But what makes everyone shudder when thinking about driving students in personal vehicles is that we will not enjoy the additional protection of professional liability insurance, hold harmless laws, or even governmental immunity (if otherwise available). These additional layers of protection are extremely valuable. Assume you pack a team of eight student athletes into the back of your van for a trip to a school across town. You are momentarily distracted, and the crash that follows results in fatalities and severe injuries among the surviving members of your team. The potential judgment against you for a moment of driving negligence would most likely exceed your policy limits if you were not covered by your employer.

The admonition, "Never drive students in your car," is a good one but you need to understand why. First, driving with a carload of students can create distracting circumstances and increase the chance of an accident. Second, driving with a carload of students is often an *ultra vires* activity that removes important layers of protection from you if an accident occurs.

It is important to understand that those extra layers of protection are not always lost to you when you drive students. For example, if you are driving students in your car to a school-sanctioned activity and your supervisor at the school has officially sanctioned you to use your car to transport the students to the event, the protections that would emanate from the school for non-*ultra vires* activities, such as hold harmless laws, continue to apply. The prudent driver, however, would be certain to get the supervisor to put the sanction in writing. The list is not short of people who have had verbal sanction from a supervisor only to find after an accident that the sanction "never occurred."

Are you safe from liability if you use the school vehicle instead of your own? Not always. It depends whether the specific use of the vehicle is a sanctioned use or an *ultra vires* use. For example, if you used the school van to move furniture from your old apartment to your new apartment, the use of the van would be *ultra vires* and all liability would be yours to bear.

Organizations' Liability Insurance

Organizations such as sports federations, clubs, and leagues often carry liability insurance. When a coach or employee asks, "Am I covered?" he or she may receive an affirmative answer grounded in a fatal misunderstanding. The organization is saying, "Yes, we are protected from claims based on your negligence." The coach or employee is hearing, "Yes, you are protected from claims against you for your negligence." The first is often correct; the second is unlikely to be correct.

Most organizations will not indemnify their employees or volunteers through the vehicle of liability insurance simply because it costs too much. All the organization will do is protect *itself* from the negligence of an employee or volunteer. So if you have such a conversation with your organization, ask for a copy of the pertinent part of the policy, and read it so that you will know if what the organization thinks it's saying is correct or what you think you are hearing is correct.

Hold Harmless Laws

Many states include public school and public college or university employees in the city or state's hold harmless laws. Although there are jurisdictional differences, hold harmless laws generally provide that the city or state will defend teachers (and often others such as coaches and administrators) in any lawsuit filed against them relating to ordinary negligence that arose out of the performance of their duties. Unlike professional liability insurance, the benefit of hold harmless laws is that they don't cost you anything. Like professional liability insurance, hold harmless laws won't protect you against charges of gross negligence or intentional acts such as defamation and discrimination.

Hold harmless laws will not apply to you if you work for a parochial school or youth sports program. They won't apply to you if you work for a charitable organization such as Girls Inc. or the Boy Scouts. But hold harmless laws are an extremely important layer of protection for teachers in public educational institutions. Check your state's laws concerning its version of hold harmless laws and see if it applies to you.

Waivers

The term "waiver" is often erroneously interchanged with "release," "agreement to participate," and "parental permission."

A release is an agreement made *after* an injury has occurred. A release relieves the potential defendant from potential liability due to the injury. A release is a contract. The consideration for the contract is usually a sum of money paid to the injured party who, in return, gives a promise to forgo any attempt to sue. Because a release is a contract, can a minor be bound by a release? No. A minor can always void a contract, including a contract in the form of a release. Nor can a minor be bound by a parent's signature on a release for an injury to the minor child. The parent can sign away any parental right to sue, but not the minor's independent right to sue.

An agreement to participate is used to inform a participant about the activity to be participated in. The agreement should describe prerequisite skills or conditioning levels, if any. It should also include a listing of the safety and behavior rules a participant is expected to exercise and the risks inherent in the activity. The agreement is informational in nature but not contractual. In fact, by itself, an agreement to participate has no legal significance. However, it is useful as evidence in a negligence case to show that the injured participant:

- assumed the risks of participation (therefore providing support for the defense called "assumption of risk" in jurisdictions acknowledging such a defense), and/or
- breached the duty owed to self to protect from foreseeable risks (risks became foreseeable because the agreement to participate listed them), therefore providing support for the defense of "comparative negligence" (or "contributory negligence" in the few states still adopting it).

Parental permission slips are not legally useful to block claims of negligence by minors. Rather, they are informational vehicles by which a parent can learn what activities a child will be engaging in and what risks are associated with that participation. The knowledge a parent might gain of the risks involved through parental permission slips is not useful in setting up an assumption of risk defense because such a defense relates to the child's assumption rather than the parent's.

Parental permission slips, however, do indicate that you have the permission of the child's parent to include the child as a participant. Such permission is particularly useful and may have legal significance for transportation, supervision, and provision of necessary medical care should such become necessary.

Now that we've spent a few moments talking about what waivers are not, let's look at what they are. Waivers are exculpatory contracts whereby a participant agrees to forgo suing you if they are injured in your program. Because waivers are contractual in nature, they carry absolutely no legal weight when signed by a minor. Remember, a minor can void contractual obligations at any time including after being injured. On the other hand, waivers are often quite useful when working with adult populations.

A waiver is enforceable if:

- it is clearly written, and
- it waives the right to sue for nothing more than ordinary negligence (i.e., not gross negligence or intentional torts), and
- it is signed by an adult for the adult's right to sue (not for a child's right to sue), and
- it is executed by parties having equitable bargaining rights.

Every now and then someone will prepare a waiver and include language which is intended to bar suit for any kind of act or omission, including gross negligence and intentional acts. Some jurisdictions will simply sift out the useless, overreaching language and enforce the remaining portion of the waiver. However, some jurisdictions will throw out the entire waiver leaving the defendant who used the waiver missing a significant layer of protection. Therefore, it seems both silly and unwise to include overreaching language in a vain attempt to protect yourself from everything when the courts will not enforce it and when, in some jurisdictions, the overreaching language destroys the entire waiver.

Waivers are limited to ordinary negligence as a matter of public policy. To allow people to exculpate themselves from liability for grossly negligent or intentional acts would create a sense of license in society that would not be in the best interests of the careful, fair behavior needed for the smooth functioning of society.

Immunity

"The King can do no wrong:" Sovereign immunity flows from the historic principle that the sovereign ruler was incapable of fault and therefore would be incapable of accepting liability.

Sovereign immunity still exists to some degree in many areas of local, state, and federal government as well as among some charitable organizations within some jurisdictions. Our ability to sue a governmental entity exists only if that right has been extended to us by specific statutory enactment that overturns the common law immunity enjoyed by governmental entities.

The doctrine of sovereign immunity is being eroded but still exists in varying degrees in many jurisdictions. Thus you should check your own jurisdiction for the degree of its application. While you're checking, be sure to note how immunity applies in your state to the various roles and levels of policy-making decisions you might be involved in.

Some states have recently adopted legislation giving immunity to individuals who are carrying out specific sports-related functions. Although this type of immunity is unrelated to "sovereign immunity," it is nonetheless important. A scarcity of youth sport coaches is being experienced in some states. In order to entice, or at least remove a barrier to, the participation of volunteer coaches of youth sports, state legislatures in well over a dozen states have enacted legislation that protects the volunteer (nonscholastic) coach from claims based on ordinary negligence.

These immunity statutes for nonscholastic coaches are similar to hold harmless statutes for teachers in that they cover only ordinary negligence in the furtherance of the coach's duties. The immunity statutes are dissimilar to the hold harmless statutes in that they do not carry any provision for defending against the claims, but rather only convey a total defense. Therefore, the youth sport coach accused of ordinary negligence must still pay for the defensive application of the immunity statute. Immunity from ordinary negligence or even innocence is not free in the context of immunity for youth sport coaches.

Not every nonscholastic coach within jurisdictions having the immunity laws is covered. Some jurisdictions require at least some low level of certification of competence by the coach in order to allow the coach to enjoy the benefits of immunity. Immunity laws sound good from the coach's standpoint. But from the standpoint of the athlete injured by a coach's negligence, they are very frustrating. It is truly a situation in which the state legislatures have had to balance the interests of society in having accessible youth sports programs against the loss to a specific athlete injured by a coach's negligence. What do you think about the balance?

Good Samaritan Laws

If we were strolling in a park and noticed that someone was drowning in the lake bordering the path, we would generally have no legal duty to assist. (A few states have enacted statutes requiring a bystander to assist in certain circumstances, but these are the exception rather than the rule.) We could continue our stroll, we could stand and ponder how many times the victim would shout "Help," but we would be under no legal obligation to assist or to even seek assistance. Certainly, the moral ramifications of inaction are significant, but the legal ones are scant.

State legislatures all across the country have tried to encourage individuals who have no duty to help, to help anyway. The term applied to statutes enacted to encourage people to help are referred to as Good Samaritan laws. Generally, Good Samaritan laws give immunity from claims of ordinary negligence made later by the victim against one who, without a duty to do so, helps. Some state's Good Samaritan laws are very inclusive, whereas others are very narrow. You should check your own state's legislation before you assume that Good Samaritan laws provide you with a layer of protection.

In no case do Good Samaritan laws protect someone who has a duty. A doctor cannot be protected by the Good Samaritan laws for ordinary negligence within the doctor's office (a duty exists between doctor and patient within the context of the doctor's office). Similarly, a teacher would not be covered by Good Samaritan laws with respect to the teacher's students at school. A teacher might be protected (depending on the particular jurisdiction) if, while not in a teacher's role, the teacher happened to find a student from the class drowning in the park's lake.

Assumption of Risk

Most jurisdictions (but not all, e.g., Pennsylvania) allow the defendant to use a defense called "assumption of risk." The elements the defendant must show in order to successfully use the assumption of risk defense are:

- **knowledge** and understanding of the nature of the risks by the participant, and
- **voluntary** consent, either expressed or implied by the participant.

Assumption of risk, when used successfully, is a total bar to the plaintiff's claims of negligence, but it is a defense of some dispute. Some view it as simply a precursor to comparative or contributory negligence. The notion behind such a view is that once we know and understand the risk, we are obligated to ourselves to protect ourselves from the foreseeable risk of unreasonable harm. If we go ahead and participate, knowing the risks, we have assumed the risks (read "duty"), thus we relieve our teachers and coaches of their duties to protect us from foreseeable risks. If we fail to protect ourselves, we have breached the duty we owe ourselves and thus might be comparatively (or contributorily) negligent.

Others view the defense of assumption of risk as a more independent concept whereby once someone knows the risks and voluntarily consents to go ahead anyway, any injury arising out of those known risks cannot be laid at the door of the teacher or coach by claiming negligence. Thus assumption of risk becomes a total bar to recovery for injuries resulting from the known and consented-to risks.

Still others view it narrowly by defining the risk which is being assumed to be only those risks which are inherent in the activity rather than the risk of negligence on the part of those people related to the activity.

Which ever view your state adopts, helping students and athletes understand the risks is valuable from a pedagogical standpoint, even if not always from a legal standpoint. The use of risk statements is one way of developing the assumption of risk defense.

Beginning swimming students have the pedagogical right to know what risks are involved if they dive into the shallow end, run on the deck, or even do everything right. A broken neck from diving in the shallow end, injuries from slipping on the deck, and chlorine irritation of the eyes are all risks of swimming. Yes, some of the risks only exist if safety rules are broken, but there are others, such as the chlorine irritation, which are just part of the activity. From a pedagogical perspective, participants who know and understand the risks yet proceed anyway can assist in protecting themselves against the known risks. From a legal perspective, participants who know and understand the risks yet voluntarily decide to participate anyway are, in many jurisdictions, less likely to be able to put legal blame for incurring those risks on others.

The second element of the assumption of risk defense, voluntary consent, can be lost if the teacher or coach forces participation, either overtly or covertly. There is broad jurisdictional variance in viewing the element of voluntary consent. In some states, even the techniques of the manipulative encouragement employed by some coaches and teachers might be sufficient to destroy the voluntary nature of a consent.

The legal effect of risk statements varies widely from jurisdiction to jurisdiction because the validity and interpretation of the affirmative defense of assumption of risk varies widely from jurisdiction to jurisdiction. For instance, to what level of consciousness does someone need to know and understand the risks?

In Pennsylvania, for instance, a plaintiff must subjectively know and understand the full impact of the risks. This subjective standard makes it difficult for a defendant to demonstrate the required element of knowing and understanding the risk. The defendant would have to demonstrate that the plaintiff truly understood what it would be like to live the remainder of life as a quadriplegic or as someone without sight.[2]

Other states, such as New York, use the objective standard. The objective standard is much easier to meet because it calls for the showing of what the normal person of like age and experience would have known about the risks rather than what the specific plaintiff knew.

---

[2] Large judgments against defendants in cases in which the assumption of risk defense has been unsuccessfully used have encouraged some people to believe that a detailed, graphic explanation of all possible consequences is always required to safeguard the teacher or coach. Such is not the case. Before deciding how detailed your risk statement needs to be, first consider the pedagogical benefits. Then review your jurisdiction's concept of assumption of risk. Less detail is needed in states using the objective test and more in states using the subjective test.

Comparative and Contributory Negligence

Self-directed negligence on the part of the victim may be used defensively by a defendant in a negligence case. The defendant says, "Yes, I was negligent, but so was the participant. The plaintiff should have to bear some responsibility for self-directed negligence." In those few states still following the pure doctrine of *contributory* negligence, the plaintiff who has breached a duty to self is totally barred from recovery.

In the majority of states which follow the more modern approach of *comparative* negligence, self-directed negligence results in only a diminution of the amount to be recovered. For instance, if the jury decides that the plaintiff's self-directed negligence was responsible for 30 percent of the injury, and the judgment for the entire injury amounts to $100,000, the plaintiff will only receive $70,000. In comparative negligence there is an apportionment of the damages between the negligent defendant and the negligent plaintiff.

Accident or incident reports, if well-written and correctly used, can provide a useful vehicle for documenting self-directed negligence and thus assist in setting up the after-the-fact defense of comparative or contributory negligence. For instance, statements concerning safety rules violated by the injured student might be useful.

Whatever layers of protection are available, the first step to be taken in avoiding liability is to provide safe programs. The second step is to enlist the efforts of the participant in maintaining a safe situation by making the participant aware of the risks involved in participation. Additional risk management techniques for causes of action other than negligence are found in Chapter 14.

Memory Testers

1. Multiple Choice. Which of the following risk-shifting techniques would theoretically be most economical for the defendant in a negligence case?

   a. professional liability insurance
   b. hold harmless law
   c. assumption of risk

d. comparative negligence

e. waiver

2. Multiple Choice. Who among the following would be most likely to avail himself or herself of the Good Samaritan defense to a claim of negligence?

a. a junior high school physical education teacher whose student is injured in class

b. an athletic trainer who incorrectly treats an injury for one of the school's athletes

c. a volunteer coach for an after-school team whose athlete is injured

d. a bystander who is watching a college softball game and negligently helps someone who has fallen in the parking lot after the game.

3. True/False. Assumption of risk is a defense which would work better in a required physical education class than in an after-school athletic program.

4. True/False. Hold harmless laws protect all teachers.

5. True/False. In order to use the defense of contributory or comparative negligence effectively, the plaintiff must also be negligent.

Memory Tester Discussion

1. B. Hold harmless. All the other defenses listed involve some outlay of money, even by the innocent plaintiff. For instance, professional liability insurance involve the payment of premiums and using assumption of risk, comparative negligence or waivers as defenses involves at-trial activities of an attorney. Attorneys serving the defendant do not work on a contingency fee basis, as do plaintiff attorneys, simply because when victorious, the defendant does not win anything from which a contingency fee could be taken. So anytime you get to trial in your defense, someone must pay the attorney. Those who are fortunate to be covered by hold harmless laws will have the

expenses of the attorney paid for them as well as any damages which might be called for if found guilty of ordinary negligence in the furtherance of the employer's interests.

2. D.   Good Samaritan laws do *not* protect anyone who already owes a duty to the injured person.

3. False.   One of the two required elements for assumption of risk is the voluntary consent to participate in a particular activity. The nature of a required physical education class would defeat the voluntary nature of the consent and thus also defeat the use of assumption of risk as a risk-shifting mechanism.

The issue of voluntariness is even more fragile than the overtly mandatory nature of a required class. In many jurisdictions, for instance, if an athlete knows that participation in a specific activity is an unwritten, unspoken prerequisite for team membership, assumption of risk would not be a useful defense for the coach because the student has only two choices: participate or don't make the team.

One Pennsylvania case[3] which illustrates the fragility of voluntariness involved an athlete who was injured while playing jungle ball (full contact football without protective equipment) while trying out for the football team. Participation in the jungle ball game was an unwritten requirement for those students who wanted to be considered for team membership, and thus the athlete had no real choice to avoid injury except to withdraw from consideration for the team. The court determined that the presence of that limited choice defeated any voluntariness of the athlete's decision to participate.

---

[3] *Rutter v. Northeastern Beaver County School District,* 437 A2d 1198 (1981).

4. False.   Hold harmless protections are created by statutes, so the benefits of hold harmless laws are extended only to those specific classes of employees enumerated in the language of the statute. The benefits are typically *not* extended to private or parochial school teachers.

5. True.   Contributory or comparative negligence defenses say, in effect, "Yes, I was negligent, but so were you."

How About Looking Up a Case?

Morgan v. State of New York, 90 NY 2d 471, 685 N.E. 2d 202, 662 NYS 421 (1997). This Court of Appeals case includes a series of fact patterns and a complete and enlightening discussion of the court's application of the assumption of risk doctrine to sport-related cases.

Chapter 7
Intentional Torts:
"I Meant to Do That"

If someone hits your knee with a rubber mallet, your foot will kick forward. Such movement is not intended, even if your foot contacts someone. In order for someone to be found guilty of an intentional tort, the plaintiff must prove the defendant acted volitionally (or at least purposely failed to act when having a duty to act).

The concept of intent sounds straightforward, but legal scholars do not agree on an exact definition. There seems to be general agreement though, that the concept of intent has three elements:

- **voluntary act** (or inaction),
- **realization** of the consequences rather than the act, and
- understanding that the consequences are the logical and likely **results** of the act.

Unintentional torts do not require any of the three elements of an intentional tort. To the contrary, the required elements of the *un*intentional tort of negligence (discussed in Chapter 5) are:

- duty
- breach
- cause
- harm

None of the elements of negligence includes any notion of mind-set or even awareness of consequences. On the other hand, intentional torts, such as defamation, battery, false imprisonment, and intentional interference with a contractual right (discussed in Chapter 10), all require a mind-set that includes a desire for the act to result in the consequences.

Intentional Tort: Defamation

Defamation is a generic term used widely these days to include the older terms of slander and libel. Slander refers to spoken words and libel to written words, both of which are false and which hold the subject of the statement up to public ridicule.

In the "old days," slander was not as serious as libel because the written word had a longer life and greater impact than the spoken word. Today with television and radio, the spoken word can reach millions of ears and carry great and lasting impact. Thus today the distinction between slander and libel is of little or no significance in most jurisdictions.

Defamation's required elements are:

- a **false** statement that is
- "published" to a **third party**, which
- holds the subject up to public **ridicule**, and thereby causes
- financial **loss**.

Have You Defamed Someone Today?

1. You tell Pat that Chris is a thief. Chris is currently doing time for robbery.

2. Lee, another faculty member, is obnoxious and a poor teacher. You tell Lee privately exactly what you think, plus you add that Lee has the personality of a child molester.

3. Pat, one of your assistant coaches, is applying for a job as head coach at a rival school. You have found Pat to be an excellent coach in all respects. You are pathologically insecure about your own ability to out-coach Pat, and so you call up the athletic director at the rival school and say that Pat is always late to practice and doesn't know the rules of the game. (This is the only scenario that meets the required elements for defamation.)

If what you say is true, you cannot be found guilty of defamation. Truth is a total defense to defamation, even if what you say is nasty and hurtful.

If you say something that is false and hurtful about a particular person to that person, you cannot be found guilty of defamation because you haven't "published" your remarks to a third person. Publishing does not mean reducing your statements to a printed page. It simply means sending the words by any means to a person who is not the subject of them. You could say the words over the phone, by telegraph, by fax machine, on television or radio, or whisper them in someone's ear. All that is required to meet the element of "publish to a third party" is that you convey the remark to someone other than, or in addition to, the subject of the remark.

Most jurisdictions allow "pillow talk" between spouses (not the broader relationship implied by "significant others") to be exempt from fulfilling the element of "publishing to a third party." So if you tell lies about someone to your spouse, you are, in most jurisdictions, not guilty of defamation because you haven't published your remarks to a third person.

Defamation of a Public Person

Sometimes special circumstances, such as the victim having the status of "public person," alter the elements required to prove defamation. Public persons are those individuals who have acquired sufficient public attention to be more likely the target of comment and discussion than the rest of us. Politicians, actors, well-known athletes, and coaches, who have gained notoriety for one reason or another, are among those who would be considered "public persons." A professional athlete, a sportscaster, or a college coach of a high-profile team are all public persons or figures in relation to the concept of defamation.

When a public person wants to claim defamation, an additional element is added, for a total of five. When the fifth element joins the other four, the list is:

- a false statement that is
- "published" to a third party, which
- holds the subject up to public ridicule, and thereby causes
- financial loss, and you act with
- **malice or reckless disregard for truth**.

The task of proving the elements of defamation resides with the plaintiff, as it does in almost all circumstances.

It is not easy for a plaintiff to prove malice or reckless disregard for truth. Why then is this element added when a public person is claiming defamation? The addition is made in large measure to make it more difficult for the public figure to successfully sue for defamation. Once a person enters the public realm, that person must have somewhat thicker skin and should realize that public persons will be the target of negative comments more often than a private person.

The Golden Rule of Defamation

If you're not sure it's true, don't say it.
If you think it's true but it's negative, don't say it unless you must.

When a baseball fan at the World Series calls out "the umpire is helping the other team," the first four elements might arguably exist (if, in fact, the umpire suffered financial loss because of the statement). However, proving that the fan had malice or reckless disregard for the truth when the statement was made is difficult.

Most instances in which a teacher, coach, or administrator might be accused of defamation do not involve public figures but are more likely to involve such things as letters of recommendation for peers and students, observation reports, and casual, intemperate comments about colleagues. Probably the best rule to follow concerning defamation is: If you're not sure it's true, don't say it; if you think it's true but it's negative, don't say it unless you must.

Defamation per se

There are some false statements so damaging that society (through the judicial system) has decided the victim does not have to prove financial damages. Instead of the four standard elements required to prove defamation, defamation *per se* requires only three:

- a false statement, which is
- "published" to a third party, which
- holds the subject up to public ridicule.

No demonstration of financial loss is needed. This is because society assumes that anyone would have been damaged sufficiently to have the right to sue when false statements are made from one of the defamation *per se* categories.

Some of these category titles, though they use archaic terminology, apply today. They include statements about the plaintiff's:

- moral turpitude,
- unchastity,
- loathsome disease status, or
- professional behavior.

The definition of moral turpitude is ambiguous, but it does include most felonies such as murder, rape, and burglary. So if someone made the false statement to your boss that you were a rapist, you would not need to show financial loss in order to pursue a successful defamation suit against the maker of the statement.

The definition of unchastity varies greatly between generation and cultural groups. However, within the meaning of defamation *per se,* the definition of unchastity remains relatively conservative. If a student falsely tells another student that Chris has slept with the entire basketball team, the required elements of defamation *per se* would exist, even without a demonstration that the statement caused its victim to sustain financial loss.

Over the years the list of what might be considered loathsome diseases has enlarged. For instance, false statements that someone has AIDS would, in today's society, probably meet the elements required for defamation *per se.*

If Teacher Pat falsely told a department chairperson that Coach Chris was dishonest, Chris might be able to sue for defamation but not for defamation *per se*. On the other hand, if Teacher Pat falsely told a department chairperson that the school's accountant, Chris, was dishonest, Chris might be able to sue for defamation *per se*. This different result for Accountant Chris would occur because dishonesty goes to the core of Chris's professional life. You and I would both argue that honesty is a trait of a good teacher and most people would support us. However, the law is talking about traits central to one's professional being.

Why would a plaintiff prefer to be able to sue under the rubric of defamation *per se* rather than defamation? Proving financial loss is difficult and is often *the* most difficult element of defamation to prove. Unless the victim can show such facts as a job being lost, promotion being denied, or a client going to someone else because of the false remark, a claim of defamation will fail.

If you've ever been denied a promotion or passed over for a new job, you might have thought it happened unfairly, but you also know that proving so would be a difficult task indeed. Thus because the plaintiff in a defamation *per se* case is not required to meet this difficult task, the plaintiff has a better chance of suing successfully.

INTERIM REVIEW

Defamation by the Numbers

The four elements required for defamation are:

- a false statement
- "published" to a third party
- which holds the subject up to public ridicule
- with financial loss

The three elements required for defamation *per se* are:

- a false statement
- "published" to a third party
- which holds the subject up to public ridicule

The five elements required for defamation of a public figure are:

- a false statement
- "published" to a third party
- which holds the subject up to public ridicule
- with financial loss
- and malice or reckless disregard for truth

The four categories of statements that turn defamation into defamation *per se* are:

- moral turpitude
- unchastity
- loathsome disease
- professional behavior

Defenses to Claims of Defamation

Truth

Truth is a total defense to all claims of defamation. However, when you are asked to evaluate a peer's teaching or coaching effectiveness, a great deal of that evaluation is, by its very nature, subjective. It is especially important when your evaluation is negative to remember that it is also subjective. Proving the truthfulness of subjective evaluations is difficult, yet that would be your burden if charged with defamation. Once the plaintiff has demonstrated the four elements (assuming the plaintiff is not a public figure), the burden of defending becomes yours.

When a peer evaluation or recommendation is negative, it should be prepared in such a way as to support its subjective conclusions as much as possible. For instance, you should include specific examples of the negative behavior, thus supporting the subjective conclusion with objective data.

If you are basing your negative recommendation or evaluation on the findings or observations of others, you should take even more care to determine the objective accuracy of those negative findings or observations. Even if you base your evaluation on the findings or observations of someone else, you are the person who will have to prove their truthfulness if charged with defamation.

Privilege

Sometimes people have a privilege that allows them to do things that otherwise could result in successful lawsuits against them because of their actions. Defamation is an area of the law in which several types of privileges exist.

For instance, a judge in open court has an absolute privilege to defame someone and the defamed person is totally barred from recovery. This absolute privilege is being eroded slightly in some jurisdictions in which a few judges have turned their absolute privilege into a license to destroy reputations, but generally, the privilege is alive and well.

Teachers, coaches, and school administrators do not enjoy an *absolute* privilege as they carry out their duties. Instead if they meet specific requirements, they can avail themselves of a *qualified* privilege. The requirements that must all be met in order to avail oneself of the qualified privilege and thus protect against claims of defamation are:

- a statement made with no reason to believe it was false, and
- a statement made by someone with a reason to make it to someone with a justifiable interest in knowing.

The first requirement, that the statement (either written or spoken) must be made with the maker having no reason to believe the statement was false, is the more difficult of the two to prove. In essence it means that you should have clean hands and a pure heart. If you know or have reason to believe that your negative statement is based only on rumor or suspicion, you have probably lost your access to the qualified privilege. If you don't have a qualified privilege and the statement turns out to be false, you are in jeopardy of being successfully sued for defamation.

Assume that the personnel file for one of the teachers in your department for whom you have been asked to prepare a letter of recommendation includes notes indicating excessive absences and consistent lateness. Your experience with the individual has always been that the teacher is on time and in attendance. Would you meet the first requirement for obtaining a qualified privilege if you took the file's word for the absences and lateness? Probably not.

In order to meet the first requirement, you cannot even have a reason to *suspect* the veracity of your negative statement. In the case of the teacher being evaluated, your experience is in contrast to the file; this should be sufficient to cause you to do further research before basing negative statements on the file. If you don't check, and it turns out that the notes were misfiled and actually belong to a teacher who was fired last year, you do not have the protection of a qualified privilege when sued for defamation.

The second requirement, that the statement was made by someone with a reason to make it to someone with a right to know, is easier to meet. Most of us don't write unsolicited letters of recommendation, nor do we file official evaluation reviews when not asked to do so by our employers or by policy. But when we volunteer information that turns out to be false, even though we didn't know it was false when we said it, we have lost the qualified privilege.

To illustrate the partial privilege's second requirement, let's assume a coach thinks a player on an opponent's team is using anabolic steroids and so telephones the local sports writer to say so. The coach who does this will not enjoy the protection of a qualified privilege when it turns out that the player is not using steroids and a defamation suit is initiated. There is no qualified privilege for the coach because the newspaper was not a future employer of the player seeking a recommendation, nor did it have any other right to inquire. If the coach had no reason to believe the steroid statement was false, the coach would still lose the qualified privilege because the statement was made to an entity that did not have the right to be told. If, on the other hand, the athlete really was using steroids, there could be no successful claim of defamation because truth is a complete defense. Both requirements must be met in order to obtain the qualified privilege.

Statute of Limitations

The statute of limitations for defamation is short, typically one year. In most jurisdictions, the statute for a defamed adult begins when the victim discovers the defamation. The short statute indicates that defamation is not a favored cause of action by the courts and that delay in bringing a case makes defense of the case even more difficult.

CHALLENGE REVIEW

Defamation

1. Which statement would be better and why?

    • "Coach Lee is a rotten coach," or
    • "Coach Lee has had over 50 percent of the team refuse to play because of the coach's use of berating and abusive techniques."

2. If the star of the season's best new television sitcom is the subject of false statements, what elements would have to be proven if the star claims defamation?
3. What are the requirements that must be met by a teacher who wishes to use a qualified privilege to protect against the risk of defamation claims?
4. List the four categories of statements that convert defamation into defamation *per se*.

Common Misconceptions about Defamation

Some people think if they say false, negative things over the phone rather than putting them in writing, they haven't committed defamation. This is not true. Certainly, telephone conversations may make it less likely for the victim to prove the statement was made or even know that it was made, but the defamatory actions of the speaker are just as defamatory.

Other people, in an attempt to avoid defamation claims, decline when asked to prepare recommendations or peer reviews. This declination may be safe, but it is not always the professionally sound path to take. Peer evaluations and letters of recommendation are part of our jobs as teachers, coaches, and administrators. The absence of such evaluative processes due to fear of defamation claims leaves those who hire, promote, and make other personnel and admission office decisions without important information. To refuse to participate in the process abdicates professional responsibilities. A better and more honorable path to take, whether or not we are afraid of defamation claims, is to make certain that what we say is true. Truth defeats any defamation claim.

Recommendations solicited by the subject of the letters that contain negative statements should not come as a surprise to the subject. Therefore it is good policy, if you agree to prepare the letter and know it will include negative comments, to indicate that the subject seek someone else to write for them. Secret "black-balls" are neither fair nor professional and typically produce anger in the subject when discovered, thus increasing risk of defamation claims. Defamation claims, whether valid or not, cause the defendant to pay for a defense. Remember, hold harmless laws and professional liability insurance do not protect against intentional torts.

Memory Tester—Defamation

1. True/False. If you write an unflattering and true statement about your supervisor and put it in your supervisor's mailbox, you are guilty of defamation.

2. True/False. The statute of limitations for defamation is longer than the statute of limitations for negligence.

3. True/False. It is more difficult for the President of the United States to prove defamation when someone calls the President "stupid, dishonest, incompetent, and a liar" than it would be for you to prove defamation when someone says the same about you.

4. True/False. Any false, negative statement made by a teacher to anyone other than the subject is always actionable under a claim of defamation if financial loss exists.

Memory Tester Discussion

1. False.   If only the target of your remarks sees the letter, you have not "published" it to a third party, and there fore one of the required elements is missing. Also truth is a total defense.

2. False.   The statute of limitations for negligence is three years and for defamation one year.

3. True.   The President is a public person and so would have to show the additional element of "malice or reckless disregard for the truth."

4. False.   If the teacher has acted in good faith regarding the truthfulness of the remarks and has expressed them to someone with a right to know, the teacher will have obtained a qualified privilege.

Intentional Tort: Battery

"Battery" is a term that has use in both the civil and criminal realms of the law. The elements are slightly, but significantly, different.

In the civil realm, battery refers to any harmful or offensive intentional contact that is unprivileged or unpermitted. The intent must be to contact. In the criminal realm, battery is most frequently defined in similar ways except that the intent must be to harm.

In this chapter we will be discussing battery mainly in the civil context. Thus the elements of battery (civil) are:

- intent to contact,
- contact,
- harmful or offensive actions, and
- being unprivileged or unpermitted.

There is no requirement that the victim be injured. Rather, the only requirement relating to the result of the contact is that the contact needs to be harmful or offensive to the plaintiff. A kiss would, under some circumstances, qualify as "harmful or offensive."

Part of the Game or Violence?

In the context of sport, the intentional tort of battery is most frequently found when fair play leaves and violence arrives. The line between the two is sometimes blurred in the eyes of some sports participants. A slide into second base with spikes high, a well-placed elbow carrying a message of intimidation, or a stroke with a hockey stick higher than it needs to be are in some people's view close to the line (on one side or the other). Some people would call these actions "part of the game." Others would call them acts of violence.

More and more sport-related claims of civil battery are finding their way to court. Is this because society, through the judicial system, has decided that there is too much violence in society and that allowing it to flourish unrestricted within the context of sport is no longer tolerable? Perhaps it is because the victims of violence in sport have decided not to be victimized silently anymore. Whatever the reason, there is an increase in the number of cases.

The line between being part of the game and violence remains unclear, both in some participants' eyes and in the eyes of the court. However, if a participant violates a safety rule of the game it makes it easier for a finding of battery to exist. Some rules relate to the progress of the game and others relate to safety. In field hockey, the rule limiting the height that the stick can swing to is a safety rule rather than a rule relating to the progress of the game. On the other hand, a rule about stepping over the center line in a volleyball game is not a safety rule but a progress of the game rule.

If contact is part of the game and it happens to lead to an injury, the injured player will not be able to successfully claim battery. This is because the element of "unpermitted and unprivileged" is absent. When a player decides to play, the player consents (gives permission) to contact that is part of the game. Thus the placement of the line between violence and part of the game is critical.

Mistaken Target

When a player intends to contact one person in a harmful or offensive way but actually ends up contacting someone else by mistake, the claim of battery belongs to the person actually contacted. Mistake of target is not a defense on the part of the person doing the battery because the issue is contact, not target.

Battery by Agency

Battery claims can be lodged against someone who did not actually do the contacting. When a coach instructs a player to "hit hard enough to take the opponent out of the game" or "remember the opponent has a bad right knee; aim for the knee," the coach is making the player an agent. Just as in negligence, responsibility for the agent's actions can be placed on the principal (in the legal sense— not the principal of the school) or, in this example, the coach.

So for many reasons, not the least of which is fear of being charged with civil battery, coaches should be careful what they ask their players to do in the heat of the game.

Battery by Teachers and Coaches

More and more teachers and coaches are finding themselves having to discipline and control students and athletes in potentially violent confrontations. When a teacher intervenes in a fight, removes a weapon from a student, or restrains an out-of-control student and contacts the student in the process, is the teacher guilty of battery? It depends. The paragraphs below discuss this issue in several contexts.

Corporal Punishment

Corporal punishment is certainly intentional, but is it battery? Defining corporal punishment is difficult. It is not the physical restraint of students by school officials in order to prevent physical harm to themselves and others or the destruction of property; such restraint would not be battery because it would be privileged. It is corporal punishment when a teacher paddles a recalcitrant student. It might be corporal punishment when a teacher uses more subtle behaviors, such as using excess exercise as a motivation or the discipline technique, "You're late; do 25 extra push-ups."

Most existing legal theories used in the area of corporal punishment are theories requiring extrapolation or adaptation. Constitutional theories, negligence, *in loco parentis,* and the intentional tort of civil battery are the main categories that have been employed, but they have been only marginally successful in enforcing an environment free of corporal punishment.

Constitutional theories used in corporal punishment cases. The 8th (cruel and unusual punishment) and the 14th (due process required in order to deprive someone of a liberty interest) Amendments to the U.S. Constitution are the most commonly used constitutional theories in the area of corporal punishment. When the 8th Amendment has been used, the courts have been asked to decide if the nature of a particular punishment was cruel and unusual. The courts have generally said corporal punishment is not cruel and unusual. When the 14th Amendment has been used, the courts have been asked to decide if the victim's right to due process prior to the infliction of corporal punishment was violated. The courts have generally said that the infliction of corporal punishment requires little, if any, due process. Historically, neither the 8th nor 14th Amendment has been particularly successful as used by victims of corporal punishment. (Chapter 12 has a discussion of constitutional theories.)

In loco parentis.　For decades the use of reasonable corporal punishment was upheld by the courts on the basis of the theory of *in loco parentis*. This refers, in part, to the privilege of the teacher to act as a parent in disciplining students while the students are engaged in school activities. If a punishment technique would be acceptable or reasonable if used by a parent, that technique would also be acceptable if a teacher or coach used it. The corporal punishment delivered to the student would not have been battery because it was privileged.

Today, the basic notion of *in loco parentis* has been diminished. The source of the privilege to punish or discipline is viewed less as flowing from the parent's delegation to the school and more as flowing from the state via compulsory education laws and therefore from the state's obligation to maintain discipline in the educational environment.

Negligence as a claim in corporal punishment cases.　Teachers and coaches have the duty to protect from foreseeable risk of unreasonable harm. If corporal punishment in the form of excess exercise (such as extra laps or push-ups) causes harm, it is theoretically possible to use negligence as a theory against corporal punishment's results, but few students have used it successfully.

Battery as a theory against corporal punishment.　When battery is used as the legal theory in a corporal punishment case, the focus of discussion is on the element requiring a showing of "unpermitted and unprivileged contact." Certainly, in the typical "paddling" corporal punishment case, the teacher or coach intended a contact that was harmful or offensive. If the student can show that the contact was unpermitted or unprivileged, the case for battery will have been made.

Students don't give permission for corporal punishment. But does the teacher or coach have a privilege to discipline using corporal punishment? The courts have generally said "yes" to this question. At the same time, however, the courts have increasingly narrowed what is considered reasonable. Historically, teachers or coaches have been privileged to use harmful or offensive contact that was reasonably believed to be necessary for the student's proper control, training, or education.[1]

Statutory prohibitions against corporal punishment. Today the majority of states have banned the use of corporal punishment in schools. California has gone one step further and has included the use of excess exercise, such as running laps or doing push-ups as punishment, as corporal punishment. A teacher who violates specific state legislation against corporal punishment may find it difficult to defend a claim of battery lodged by the student.

Even though teachers and coaches in some jurisdictions continue to have the right to use corporal punishment to some degree, the issue still remains: How much or what intensity of force is reasonably believed to be necessary? If reasonableness is exceeded, no privilege is bestowed.

Self-Defense as a Defense Against Battery

Sometimes a teacher or coach is involved in an altercation with a student or between students when trying to break up a fight. We've just talked about the use of reasonable force in privileged situations. How far does that privilege extend?

Can the teacher punish a student who struck the teacher by hitting the student back and still maintain the privilege? No. Self-defense is not revenge or punishment. The legal definition of self-defense is the use of reasonable force under the specific circumstances to repel the reasonably perceived threat of imminent violence.

Thus *any* hit that is delivered as punishment will not be considered self-defense. Teachers and coaches who allow their anger or frustration to direct their behaviors in ways that include the physical punishment of students or athletes are unlikely to be able to successfully claim self-defense when charged with battery.

---

[1] See, for example *Ingraham v. Wright*, 430 US 651.

Criminal Battery and Assault

Terminology varies, but many of us hear the term "assault" and we think of someone intending to hurt someone else, not just intending to contact them. In some jurisdictions the term applied to such an intention to hurt is *assault* and in others it is *criminal battery*. Whatever term is applied, the elements are generally the same as for civil battery with one exception.

The elements of criminal battery are:

- intent to *hurt*
- contact,
- harmful or offensive actions, and
- being unprivileged or unpermitted.

As our society appears to become more violent in nature, more teachers, coaches, and administrators will face issues surrounding assault or criminal battery. Criminal battery or assault may come in a variety of forms, including child abuse, third party actions by uninvited persons on campus, school fights, and fights on the field of play. Jurisdictional details vary greatly, but jail time is frequently tied by statute to acts of criminal battery or assault.

Athletes injured by the intent of their opponents, both in the scholastic and professional realms, are more frequently pursuing criminal charges against the perpetrator. Teachers, coaches, and administrators are more frequently being charged with negligence for failing to prevent injury to their students and athletes by those who would criminally batter or assault. Although schools may be safer than the media portray, the increasing presence of gangs and outsiders on campus also increases the foreseeability of unreasonable injury at the hands of those intending to hurt, thus placing a duty on the teachers, coaches, and administrators to act in prudent, reasonable, up-to-date ways to avoid having their students injured.

Intentional Tort: False Imprisonment

False imprisonment does not refer to incarceration in the nearest jail. Instead it means that someone is, without privilege or permission, intentionally denying your right to go where you want to go.

Suppose a friend came over for dinner, and after dinner you started setting up the slide projector intending to show a few hours of your best slides from your summer vacation. The friend wanted to leave but you locked the doors and swallowed the key. You are guilty of false imprisonment, as well as a significant breach of manners. If, instead of swallowing the key, you had used or even implied a threat, the same would be true.

If a patron in your pro shop at a fitness center started to leave the shop carrying a tennis racket you thought the patron had shoplifted from your shop, could you detain the patron until the police arrived without threat of losing a false imprisonment lawsuit? Yes, if your suspicion turned out to be correct.

Now let's assume the same facts except that the tennis racket actually belonged to the patron. Could you detain the patron until the police arrived without threat of losing a false imprisonment lawsuit? The answer in this version of the scenario depends on your particular jurisdiction. A number of states have enacted legislation generically referred to as the "shopkeeper's privilege." One of the elements of false imprisonment is that the detention be unprivileged. The shopkeeper's privilege provides the shopkeeper with the privilege to detain and, in fact, retrieve a shopper while defeating claims of false imprisonment if the patron turns out to be innocent. However, all of the following elements must be present for the shopkeeper to obtain the privilege. The shopkeeper must:

- have reasonable suspicion,
- detain for only a reasonable period of time,
- use only reasonable force, and
- retrieve from only a reasonable distance.

So if a shopkeeper has reasonable suspicion (not liking the way someone looks is insufficient to meet this element) to believe a patron has shoplifted, the shopkeeper can retrieve the patron, using reasonable force (never deadly force), even from the parking lot, and detain the patron until the police arrive (assuming the police were promptly called).

If your jurisdiction has adopted a shopkeeper's privilege, it should be used with care. Claims of defamation can still be made against you if you retrieve or detain the patron in a manner including accusations making it apparent to all others in the store that you are calling the patron a thief. You would also be wise to wait for the police to search the belongings of the patron, thus avoiding all varieties of accusations against you, including theft, sexual abuse, and so on.

Risk Management for Intentional Torts

The main risk management tool for intentional torts is summarized in the phrase, "Just don't do it." The logic of public policy says that if people who intended to harm or injure others were allowed to shift liability for their evil intent to an insurance company or other entity, they would be less likely to curb their evil intentions. This would not be a good result for society.

Therefore, hold harmless laws and other types of defenses in *un*intentional torts, do not cover intentional torts. This prohibition includes professional liability insurance policies. Insurance companies will generally *not* pay for *liability* arising out of intentional torts such as sexual harassment, false imprisonment, and defamation, but a closer reading reveals that the protection does *not* include the payment of any damages, only the cost of defense for a plaintiff who is ultimately found to be innocent.

How About Looking Up a Few Cases?

If you're near a law library, you might find it interesting to read some of the following cases. Some have value as precedents within their jurisdictions, others don't. Don't assume that the outcome would be the outcome in your jurisdiction. However, read the cases to gain an insight into how the issues of intentional torts are evaluated. As you read them, develop arguments of your own for the plaintiff and then for the defendant. If you are using the Internet to find cases, check the Appendix for suggested sites.

> *Hackbart v. Cincinnati Bengals*, 435 F. Supp. 352 (1977), rev'd. 601 F 2d 516 (1979), cert. denied 444 U.S. 931, 100 S. Ct. 275 (1979). This case involving professional football players considers the issue of "part of the game."

> *Ingraham v. Wright*, 430 US 651. This is a landmark case in the area of corporal punishment.

Nabazny v. Barnhill, 31 Ill. App ad 212, 334 N.E. 2d 258 (1975). This is one of the classic cases on sport violence and claims of battery.

Tomjanovich v. California Sports, Inc., No. H-78-243 (S.D. Texas Aug. 17, 1979). Also, more readily available in 16 Akron Law Review 537 (Winter, 1983). Tomjanovich, a professional basketball player, was intentionally injured by a fellow player. The case makes interesting reading and highlights the issues of battery in sport.

Chapter 8
Contracts:
"Put It in Writing"

Most contractual relationships fall into one of two main categories: personal service contracts and contracts for goods. This chapter will deal with the general concepts involved in contractual obligations. Chapter 9 will discuss contracts for the selling and purchasing of goods, and Chapter 10 will discuss contracts for personal service in which one person agrees to work for another.

The obligations or reciprocal promises that are created when people enter into any contract are defined by the parties. Bargaining and negotiating produce the reciprocal responsibilities that each party to a contract owes to the other. If you don't like the price of a new volleyball, you walk away.

Elements of a Contract

Specific requirements must exist in order for a contract to be enforceable by the courts. These elements are as follows:

- There must be a **meeting of the minds** between the buyer and the seller.

- The subject of the contract must be a **legal subject.**
- There must be an **offer.** There must be an **acceptance,** either by word or deed.
- Some form of **consideration** must be involved.
- The parties must have the **legal capacity** to enter into a contract.
- The terms of the contract must be sufficiently **precise.**

Meeting of the Minds

In order for a contractual relationship to exist, there must be an understanding or meeting of the minds of the parties. If you think you are purchasing volleyballs and the seller thinks you want basketballs, there is no contract even if you agree on the price, because there is no meeting of the minds. After all the bargaining and negotiating, both the buyer and the seller must understand and agree to their own obligations and the obligations of the other.

Legal Subject

If a contract is made to perform some illegal act or purchase some illegal merchandise, that contract is not enforceable by the courts. I'm not sure who would be dumb enough to ask the court to enforce a contract to shave points in a championship game or to purchase anabolic steroids, but if someone did try to gain the court's help in enforcing such a contract, that person would be unsuccessful.

Offer and Acceptance

In order for a contract to exist, there must be both an offer to sell by the seller and an acceptance of that offer by the buyer. This seems so simple that it doesn't need to be said, yet many of the contract cases that find their way to courts involve the question of whether there was an offer and an acceptance.

Is this an offer?
1. A sporting goods dealer says to you, "I'll bet I could get you those uniforms for $30 each."
2. A sporting goods dealer says to you, "I'll sell you 20 of those uniforms for $30 each."

Is this an acceptance?
1. You tell a sporting goods dealer, "If our school makes the NCAA Final Four we will buy 20 uniforms at $30 each."

2. You tell a sporting goods dealer who has offered to sell you 10 composition covered volleyballs at $10 each, "We accept your offer, but please make the covers leather."

Other common questions concerning offers and acceptances that frequently arise are as follows:

Are catalogs offers?   We act as though a catalog is a list of offers, but in most situations it is not. Our acceptance of a catalog's typographically erroneous price does not obligate the seller to sell the merchandise at that price because the catalog is only an invitation to make an offer. When we send in an "order," we are really only offering to buy something at the price listed in the catalog. The seller may then accept our offer or reject it. If our offer is accepted, the seller can convey that acceptance to us by words or by deeds. Thus the acceptance can be perfected when the seller gives us confirmation of the order and its accepted terms or by merely shipping our order.

How long is an offer in force?   Unless the person making the offer says otherwise, an offer stays open and is capable of being accepted for a "reasonable" period of time. If the offeror specifies, "This offer is good only until midnight, January 14," the offer will not be capable of being accepted on January 15 even if the offer had not been in force a reasonable period of time by its expiration at midnight January 14.

Even though an offer is usually considered open for a reasonable period of time, it can be affirmatively revoked at any time, including a time earlier than the expiration of the reasonable period of time. However, that early revocation must be conveyed to a potential acceptor before the revocation is valid. In other words, if you accept an offer and the offeror says, "I decided to revoke that offer yesterday but didn't tell you," your acceptance is valid and a contract exists in spite of the offeror's protests.

What is an option?   An option is a separate contractual arrangement whereby the potential buyer pays the seller a specific sum so that the seller will hold the offer open for a specific period of time for the potential buyer. The reciprocal promises made in an option contract are:

1. The offeror promises to hold the offer open for a specified period of time for the potential buyer, and

2. The offeree promises to pay a specified sum to the offeror for the offeror's promise.

What happens if either the offeror or the offeree backs out of the option? If the offeror or seller decides not to sell the item during the term of the option, that's too bad for the offeror or seller. The seller is obligated to sell the item to the offeree or buyer during the option period. An option means that the buyer is guaranteed that the purchase can be made for the period of time for which the option was purchased.

If the offeree or buyer decides not to buy during the term of the option, that's okay. All the buyer will lose is the money spent on the option.

Does the use of unsolicited goods constitute an acceptance and thus obligate the user to pay for the goods? No. The technique of sending someone unsolicited goods is less popular now than in the past, but it still creates confusion concerning the existence of an obligation to pay for the goods.

If a seller of sporting goods mails an unsolicited warm-up suit to you and you wear it, you are not obligated to pay for the suit when a bill later arrives. Neither are you obligated to return the suit. Unsolicited goods may be considered gifts by the recipient. You can elect to keep them or return them, but you have no obligation to pay for them. Why? You have no obligation to pay because you have not entered into a contract.

Consideration

In most contracts, consideration means the exchange of something of value. If you enter into a contract to buy field hockey sticks, the money you pay for them becomes the consideration.

If there is no consideration, there is no contract. That doesn't mean that a contract fails to exist just because you failed to keep your promise to pay for the hockey sticks. It does mean that if there was never any promise to pay for them, there would never have been a contract in the first place. If you promised but failed to carry out your promise, you would have breached the contract, and the seller could enlist the court's aid in enforcing your obligations under the contract.

If you said to someone, "I volunteer to coach the youth softball team" and you failed to do so, you may have broken the young athletes' hearts and appeared irresponsible, but you would not have broken a contract. In the absence of consideration given on the part of the youth sports team or league (such as a promise to pay you for coaching or a promise to arrange college credit for you as a student coach), there is no contract.

Legal Capacity

Minors can make enforceable contracts, but minors cannot be the subject of contractual enforcement. This means that a contract with a minor is voidable by the minor, but it is not void from the outset. If the minor later has a change of mind, the minor can void the contract, and the other party cannot enforce the minor's promises and obligations (except for necessaries such as food and shelter). The enforcement of contracts with minors is a one-way street. Such contracts are only enforceable by the minor. Therefore, it is very risky to make contracts with minors.

Let's assume that your high school's athletes want to order letter jackets with their names embroidered on the front and you generously offer to place a group order with the supplier of the jackets. After the jackets arrive, Pat, one of the athletes, says the jacket idea is no longer appealing and refuses to pay you for the jacket. Can you force Pat to pay?

No. Pat is a minor and Pat has elected to void a contract that was, from the outset, voidable. Unless your name is Pat, you will have a useless jacket to serve as a reminder of the legal truth that contracts with minors are voidable. Pat's jacket will also remind you that it would have been a better idea to make your jacket purchase arrangements with the parents of the athletes rather than with the athletes. If the parents changed their minds about purchasing the jacket, you would be able to enforce their promise to pay.

As we've discussed above, contracts with minors are voidable,[1] but so are contracts with severely retarded individuals or insane[2] persons due to their lack of legal capacity (the capacity to understand the contractual process). A voidable contract can be enforced

---

[1] Exculpatory agreements or contracts, such as waivers with minors, are problematic because of the minor's ability to void such contracts at any time, including after an injury. The use of waivers is discussed in Chapters 6 and 14.

[2] Contracts with the insane used to be considered void, but now they are generally considered voidable.

by the party lacking legal capacity but not by the other. A void contract cannot be enforced by either party.

Specificity of Terms

If the parties to a contract inadvertently are vague about the price or quantity of goods to be purchased, the contract might fail unless the parties can later agree, or if not, the court can fill in the blanks with some degree of certainty. For instance, if uniforms were ordered for the "team" but no specific number was indicated, the court might feel comfortable in deciding that the number of uniforms to be purchased was the same as the number of athletes on the roster.

However, the failure of the parties to be precise about material terms including price and quantity often dooms the contract. If the failure of the contract is discovered after the uniforms are used and the courts cannot fill in the blanks, it would be unfair to the seller to announce that no contract ever existed for lack of specificity. The seller would receive back used uniforms and no payment for them. In order to avoid such unfair results, the court in such circumstances may apply the equitable relief of *quantum meruit. Quantum* (amount) *meruit* (deserved) is a legal principle that allows the court to determine not what the contract would have said, but rather what is the value of the benefit, goods, or services received. The court determines this amount and then orders the recipient of the benefit, goods, or services to pay it to the provider. The existence of the legal principle of *quantum meruit* provides for a degree of fairness in the face of a fatally imprecise contract.

> ## Elements of a Contract
>
> In order for a contract to exist, six elements must be found:
>
> - Meeting of the minds
> - Legal subject
> - Offer and acceptance
> - Consideration
> - Legal capacity of parties
> - Precise terms

When Something Goes Wrong with a Contractual Relationship

When a contract exists but one party to the contract fails to carry out the promises made, the contract is said to be breached. There are two levels of breach: immaterial and material. If a breach is immaterial, its existence does not cause the rest of the contract to fail.

If, for example, the contract calls for the goods to be shipped by United Parcel Next Day Air and the seller instead ships via Federal Express Next Day Air, the breach would be immaterial. If a personal service contract calls for a teacher to start class at 9AM, yet three times during the term the teacher starts the class late at 9:03 AM, the breach would also be immaterial.

Can you think of breaches which would be material? How about if, instead of sending the package by either Federal Express or United Parcel Next Day Air, the seller let the goods sit on the loading dock for two months? How about if, instead of starting the class a few minutes late, the teacher failed to show up at all for a month? Certainly, through these extremes it is easy to evaluate what is a material and an immaterial breach, but often the courts are needed to determine the difference between less obvious alterations in expected performance of a contract.

I Want My Money Back!

Material breaches are more significant than immaterial breaches and, therefore, relieve the victim of the breach from carrying out promises made. Consider the scenario in which you ordered new uniforms for a January 14th championship game, and the contract included a clause noting that the uniforms had to be delivered by January 13th because they were needed for the 14th. The uniforms arrived on the 15th. The tardy arrival would be a material breach because the tardiness defeats the purpose of the initial contract, and it would be unfair to expect you to have to pay for uniforms that you no longer need. If, on the other hand, you did not inform the seller that the uniforms had to be delivered by a particular date, you would need to pay for the uniforms. It is fair to the seller for the buyer to be picky about a delivery date, but only if the buyer has informed the seller of the fact that time is of the essence.

Once a material breach has occurred, the victim can sue for breach of contract. The victim can either seek damages for the breach, or something called "specific performance" can be granted by a court. "Specific performance" is a legal term meaning that the party who breached the contract will be ordered by the court to fulfill the contract totally. It is not often used, but in certain types of cases, it may be of greater use to the victim than would be money damages. For example, if you contracted to purchase a particular fitness facility because it was located right next to your swimming facility, you would want the court to force the seller to specifically perform (sell you the property) rather than simply pay money damages.

In most breach of contract cases, the remedy is money damages. The amount of damages is determined by the court unless the contract has included a clause defining liquidated damages. Liquidated damages are not "fluid" or "watery" damages but rather an amount of money one party will owe to the other in the case of breach. The amount of money to be paid is determined at the time of the making of the contract, not at the time of the breach. Including a clause in the contract identifying the amount of liquidated damages often encourages both parties to meet their obligations under the contract. (The amount of liquidated damages decided on needs to bear some relation to the actual expectation of the value of a breach rather than merely to serve as a penalty for the party who breaches.) If a breach occurs, the process of determining the compensation owed the victim has already been settled.

Memory Testers—Elements of a Contract

1. True/False. If someone mails you an unsolicited new pair of sneakers and your dog chews them up, you will have to pay the sender for the shoes, even if you intended to send them back before hunger pangs overcame your canine.

2. True/False. You ordered an engraved class ring for one of your students who promised to pay you for it with next year's allowance. You can legally force the student to pay you.

3. True/False. Your teacher promises to pay you $10 if you lose 10 pounds. You don't. Your teacher can force you to lose the weight.

4. True/False. Your professor promises to pay you $10 if you stop smoking. You stop smoking but your professor doesn't pay, saying there is no consideration on your part.

5. True/False. In order to be enforceable, a contract must be in writing.

Memory Tester Discussion

1. False.   You may use or dispose of unsolicited goods in any manner without incurring the obligation to pay for them. This is true regardless of what the sender's "bill" says. If there was never a contract or there was a failed contract, there is no legal obligation to pay for unsolicited goods.

2. False.   Contracts with minors are voidable. If the student elects to void the contract, even after the ring is engraved, the contract cannot be enforced against the student.

3. False.   Assuming you are a minor, the teacher cannot enforce the contract against you.

4. False.   Consideration doesn't always mean money, goods, or even benefit to the other party. It may simply be refraining from doing something that you have a legal right to do. You have a right to smoke and you have refrained from exercising that right in response to your contractual agreement with your professor. You can enforce the contract.

     A more likely example of a contract in which one party agrees to refrain from doing something for which the party has a legal right would be a noncompete contract. For example, if you were hired as an assistant director of the Local Fitness Center and your contract included a clause saying you promised that for one year following the termination of your employment at the Local Fitness Center you would not work for any competitor within a two-mile radius of the fitness center, such a clause would be enforceable against you unless a court determined its terms were unreasonable.

5. False.   Contracts do not need to be in writing in order to be enforceable, except for a small, specific group of contracts such as contracts relating to real property. However, the terms of a verbal contract are difficult to prove. So any contract of any significance should be

reduced to writing. When a contract is made, both parties are happy. When there is a problem with a contract, at least one party is unhappy, but it is too late. So follow the axiom, "Put it in writing!"

How About Looking Up Some Cases?

If you're near a law library, you might find it interesting to read some of the following cases as well as the Uniform Commercial Code (UCC) which governs a major portion of contracts for the sale of goods. Some cases have value as precedents within their jurisdictions, others don't. So don't assume that the outcome would be the outcome in your jurisdiction. However, read them to gain an insight into how the issues of contract law are evaluated. As you read them, develop arguments of your own for the plaintiff and then for the defendant. If you're planning on using the internet to find the cases or UCC sections, check in the Appendix for suggested sites.

Bruner v. University of Southern Mississippi, 510 So 2d 1113 (Miss. 1987). This case deals with the topic of a coach acting as agent for the university.

Forbes v. Wells Beach Casino, Inc., 307 A 2d 210 (Me. 1973). This older case considers the differences between formal offers and invitations to negotiate.

Rooney v. Tyson, 91 NY2d 685, 697 N.E. 2d, 571, 674 NYS 2d 616 (1998). This case deals with the issue of an oral contract between Mike Tyson and his trainer.

Schumann v. Berg, 37 Cal 2d 174, 231 P 2d 39, 21 ALR 2d 1051 (1951). This much older case has an interesting discussion of the topic of consideration.

Uniform Commercial Code, section 2-206. This section discusses the manner of accepting an offer either through performance or through formal acceptance.

Contractual relationships generally fall into one of two main categories: personal service contracts and contracts for goods. The elements required for a valid, enforceable contract are generally the same for either category, but each category has some unique qualities beyond the elemental ones.

Contracts for the Purchase of Goods

How good is your Latin? *Caveat emptor* means that the buyer should remain vigilant and not make the potentially erroneous assumption that goods or services will be exactly what is expected. Even though *caveat emptor* is good advice, it is not always a sufficient protection for the buyer, and thus it is not the buyer's solitary safeguard in the marketplace. In an attempt to add fairness and stability to the marketplace, most jurisdictions have adopted many of the provisions of the Uniform Commercial Code (UCC).

The UCC was proposed as model legislation to produce a uniform set of rules for the merchant and buyer. Two of its provisions are of particular significance to the purchaser of goods. They are:

- implied warranty of merchantability, and
- implied warranty of fitness for a particular purpose.

Various jurisdictions have adopted only portions of the UCC. However, all states except Louisiana have adopted at least Article 2 of the UCC. Article 2 deals directly with the sale of good including the implied warranties of mechantability and fitness for a particular purpose.

According to the UCC, whenever you purchase goods from a merchant who deals in that particular type of goods, you will enjoy an implied warranty of merchantability. That means you have an unwritten but valid and enforceable warranty that whatever you buy will be acceptable within the trade for sale. Whatever you buy doesn't have to be the best, but it has to be acceptable by normal standards within the trade. So if you order a volleyball from a merchant who deals in sporting goods, and you receive a volleyball so poorly made that it bursts the first time it is used, you have a legal right to get your money back. This is because such a ball would not be deemed minimally acceptable among the sellers of volleyballs. The volleyballs need to be merchantable, not perfect. A product is "merchantable" when the following three points are met:

- passing in the trade without objection,
- fit for the ordinarily or generally intended purposes, adequately (by trade standards) contained, packaged, and labeled, and
- conforming to the promises on the container's or package's label.

The two required elements needed in order to obtain an implied warranty of merchantability are that:

- the goods were purchased from a merchant who deals in that type of goods, and
- the goods fall below the minimum quality acceptable in the trade.

Because this warranty is implied, you do not need any type of written statement from the seller concerning the existence of a warranty. In fact, the UCC implied warranty of merchantability is usually in effect even if the receipt you obtain from the seller says that the sale is made without any warranties, either expressed or implied.

The implied warranty of fitness for a particular purpose is less automatic than the implied warranty of merchantability. It requires the buyer to rely on the seller's advice about which type of merchandise would meet the needs of a particular purpose. If you told a salesperson at the local sporting goods store that you were relying on the salesperson's advice for a type of shoe which would be appropriate for playing competitive tennis and the salesperson sold you a track shoe, the required elements to trigger existence of the implied warranty of fitness for a particular purpose would have been met. The elements are:

- purchase goods from a merchant who deals in that type of goods, and
- at the time of the sale, the seller must have reason to know that the buyer was going to use the product for a particular use (rather than just the generally intended use); and that
- the buyer was relying on the seller's skill or judgment to select or furnish suitable goods for that particular purpose.

The UCC's inclusion of the implied warranty of fitness for a particular purpose should alert the shopkeeper to either train employees so they will be knowledgeable or instruct employees to refrain from offering advice about the appropriateness of a product for a particular use. This is particularly important in the area of sporting goods since the use of inappropriate products can cause significant injury.

The implied warranties of merchantability and fitness for a particular purpose are defeated when the goods being purchased are labeled "as is" or "with all faults" or similar language which would alert the buyer that there will be no implied warranties accompanying the goods being purchased. Even when implied warranties exist, the damages for which the seller might become liable if the warranties are breached may be limited by a liquidated damages clause or by a clause in the contract which limits damages. Read the fine print!

INTERIM REVIEW

Contracts for the Purchase of Goods

1.   The Uniform Commercial Code defines the general rules for the conduct of business related to the purchase and sale of goods.

2. Implied warranties of merchantability and fitness for a particular purpose are often available to the person who buys goods from a merchant who deals in such goods. When goods are purchased at a flea market or from a neighbor's basement, the UCC warranties are unlikely to apply.

3. Elements of a contract:
   • meeting of the minds,
   • legal subject,
   • offer and acceptance,
   • consideration,
   • legal capacity of parties, and
   • precise terms.

The UCC is the general rule book for contracts relating to the sale and purchase of goods. It tells us when an offer's acceptance can be successfully revoked, what happens if there is a typing error on an invoice, and what happens when the incorrect goods are shipped. If you are responsible for purchasing sporting goods, uniforms, or other merchandise, you should be familiar with the UCC's Article 2. If you are the boss of a pro shop or are involved in marketing your school's logo merchandise, you should be as familiar with Article 2 as you are with the rules of volleyball or basketball. Your future success depends on that knowledge.

Products Liability

Another legal issue related, at least in part, to contracts is products liability. When a product breaks or doesn't perform as promised, and thereby someone is injured, the legal concept of products liability arises. Products liability refers to the liability of a manufacturer to the user (or, in some cases, bystanders) if the use of its products results in personal injury or property damage.

Even though a teacher, coach, or administrator is not usually in the role of a defendant to claims of product failure, they are often involved as plaintiffs and thus should understand the three main theories by which recovery can be made. The three main theories under which recovery for product failure can be sought are:

• negligence,
• strict liability, and
• breach of warranty.

Under the first of these theories, **negligence,** the manufacturer has a duty to exercise that reasonable degree of care (standard of care) that every ordinarily prudent person would use in the designing, manufacturing, testing, inspecting, packaging, and labeling of a similar product to make it reasonably safe for use by the ordinary customer. Because the theory is negligence, the same four elements required of any negligence claim are needed: duty, breach, cause, and harm.

Are there any defenses to the negligence theory as it applies to products liability cases? Yes. If the defect that caused the injury or property damage was undiscoverable by the use of reasonable care and reasonable care was used, no negligence exists because the standard of care was met (no breach occurred).

Sometimes we are injured by products that were designed, inspected, packaged, and labeled with all due care. Negligence then is not a useful theory because there has been no breach of duty. The legal notion of **strict liability** might be a theory to provide a means of recovery in such circumstances.

Strict liability requires three elements. They are:

- the product contained a defect unreasonably dangerous to person or property,
- the defect existed at the time of sale by manufacturer, and
- the defect caused the injury.

Recovery for trampoline injuries has been sought using the theory of strict liability. Some juries have been convinced that trampolines are inherently dangerous and cannot be made safe regardless of how they are constructed, inspected, packaged, and labeled. If the jury in a trampoline case believes that the trampoline is inherently dangerous, the issue of whether the manufacturer exercised all possible care is not a defense. There are no defenses for the theory of strict liability in product failure cases.

The third theory of products liability is **breach of warranty.** Whenever an injury results because a product fails to perform in a way warranted (either expressed or implied) by the manufacturer, the purchaser can use the theory of breach of warranty to recover. For instance, if a personal flotation device is warrantied to support a person weighing 150 pounds but, in reality, sinks when a person weighing 100 pounds uses it, there has been a breach (failure) of the warranty. It is important to remember that even in the absence of expressed warranties, the purchaser may be able to use implied warranties under the UCC.

If the purchaser has altered or misused the product, all warranties may become void, and the theory of breach of warranty becomes useless. Therefore, it is important to correctly install and repair equipment according to the manufacturer's directions.

Why should you care about protecting against products liability cases? The price of equipment reflects the manufacturer's experience or projected exposure to successful products liability claims. Products liability cases against football helmet manufacturers have been responsible, at least in part, for the demise of all but a handful of helmet manufacturing companies. The increase in price of gymnastics equipment similarly reflects a passing of litigation costs along to the consumer. Teachers, coaches, and administrators can both help prevent injuries and protect the manufacturers of equipment (thereby keeping prices lower) by:

- setting up and maintaining equipment as per manufacturer's instructions, and
- disseminating warnings promulgated by the manufacturer (who has a duty to warn) concerning improper use of the equipment.

Memory Testers—Products Liability

1. True/False. There are no defenses to strict liability claims as long as all three required elements are proven.

2. True/False. Misusing or altering safety devices on equipment may bar the successful use of the breach of warranty theory in a products liability case.

3. True/False. The negligence theory, when used in a products liability case, requires the manufacturer to be responsible for any defect that could have been discovered by the use of modern scientific methods.

4. True/False. All the theories typically used in products liability cases are usable only by the purchaser, not by students and athletes.

Memory Tester Discussion

1. True.
2. True.
3. False.   The manufacturer must only use reasonable care and effort to find defects that could be located by ordinary, not extraordinary, means.
4. False.   In the early days of products liability cases, the successful claimant was the purchaser. However, over the years the theories have been expanded to include most individuals who could foreseeably be injured by a defective product, not just the purchaser.

Licensed, Logo Merchandise

Selling merchandise, including sports apparel and equipment carrying the logo of the school, is becoming a more frequent business pursuit. If you're involved in the process, you should ask yourself these questions:

1.   *Is the merchandising effort large enough or potentially profitable enough to justify retaining the services of an attorney to help protect the logo and develop specific licensing procedures when others want to use the logo?*

If you're only printing 50 T-shirts with your junior high school's name and logo to sell to fans at the last game of the year, it might be more expensive than it is worth to legally protect the logo.

On the other hand, if your college is going to the Final Four, it would be very wise to check on the status of your school's logo protection and licensing procedures. Amazingly, after winning national championships in high profile sports, several big-time sport universities have been embarrassed to discover that their logos have not been protected. The thousands of T-shirts, caps, mugs, and bumper stickers carrying the victorious school's logo brought no revenue to the school because of the institution's oversight. Oops.

2.   *Does our school want to restrict the use of our logo and thereby retain any potential profits from the sale of merchandise carrying the logo?*

(If so, consult an attorney.)

3. *Have we "borrowed or adapted" our logo from another institution without permission?*

Often logos start out very simply: a parent or school employee adapts a cute logo seen somewhere else. Initially there are no plans to sell merchandise carrying the "adapted" logo. Years go by. The program improves and expands and its fans develop an affection for the 'adapted' logo. The school now plans to merchandise goods carrying the logo. However, the school from which the logo was "borrowed" or "adapted" does not look favorably on your use of it. Oops again.

4. *Is the logo (mascot or team name) one which is offensive to others?*

Most people don't intend to offend, but nonetheless, many are offended when a lack of sensitivity or poor foresight results in a bad choice of a logo.

Some inappropriate selections will cause public relations problems, whereas others will cause expensive legal problems. We could have a philosophical discussion about the issues surrounding logo, mascot, and team name selection, but more to the point of this text is the legal impact of our choices. If we produce a hostile atmosphere by using a logo which is of sacred or cultural significance to particular religions or ethnic groups, we may invite the expense of defending a lawsuit based on religious harassment. Items such as eagle feathers (sacred to Native Americans), cartoons of an ethnic group, and references to stereotyped behaviors, such as the violent acts of scalping, may create both negative and offensive images for our programs and may create a sufficiently hostile environment for members of the particular group that lawsuits based on harassment may ensue. If, based on our expanding empathy for the bad will we are creating by our poor choice, we voluntarily elect to find more appropriate logos, we still incur the expense of redesigning and restocking merchandise. If, based on litigation, we are forced to change our logo, we incur the considerable legal expense of defending a lawsuit. In either case, the most efficient course to follow is to be careful in logo selection in the first place.

Risk Management Techniques for Contracts

The risk management techniques for contracts are quite straightforward:

- Have a written contract.
- Read the contract.
- Don't agree to a contract unless it totally reflects your agreement.
- Know your rights and responsibilities under the UCC.

How About Looking Up a Few Cases?

You might find it interesting to read some of the following cases. Some have value as precedents within their jurisdictions, others don't. So don't assume that the outcome would be the outcome in your jurisdiction. Read them to gain an insight into how the issues of contract law are evaluated. As you read them, develop arguments of your own for the plaintiff and then for the defendant. If you're planning on using the internet, check the Appendix for suggested sites.

> *Arnold v. Riddell, Inc.*, 882 F. Supp. 979 (D. Kan. 1995) This is an interesting case about the ability of a football helmet to prevent injury. Much of the products liability in sport has centered around football helmet manufacturers.

> *MacPherson v. Buick Motor Co.*, 217 NY 382, 111 N.E. 1050 (1916). This is the landmark case which opened up recovery under the theory of products liability for those beyond the very limited initial purchaser of the goods.

> *Nissen Trampoline Co. v. Terre Haute First National Bank*, 332 N.E. 2d 820, rev'd 265 Ind. 457, 358 N.E. 2d 974 (1976). The strict liability theory of product liability is discussed in this sport-related case.

> *San Francisco Arts & Athletics, Inc. et al. v. United States Olympic Committee, et al;* 483 US 522 (1987). This case deals with the USOC's attempts to block the use of its five-ring logo as well as the word "Olympic" by another group. It includes an excellent history of the USOC but also illustrates logo battles.

> *Shoshone Coca-Cola Bottling Co. v. Dolinsky*, 82 Nev 439, 420 P 2d 855 (1966). This product liability case is a classic for two reasons. First, the manufacturer's sole control over a product that turned out to be defectively manufactured may relieve the plaintiff of the need to prove that there was a lack of care in the manufacturing process. Second, although not a case involving a sports context, the case's facts are intriguing for most readers.

Chapter 10
Contracts for Personal Services: Hiring and Firing

Many of the personal service contracts involving teachers and administrators are not negotiated individually but as part of a bargaining unit. A bargaining unit is often a union or some other organized labor group. In such circumstances, the individual teacher or administrator has little input into the process except to ratify the final agreement. The teacher or administrator has previously elected the bargaining unit representatives and therefore must trust them to negotiate a favorable contract. If the teacher or administrator is unhappy with the result, the only choices are to either (1) accept the terms of the contract and vote the bargaining unit's representatives out of office at the next election, or (2) look for another job.

The employer who negotiates with bargaining units often does so through designated negotiators rather than personally. The employer in such instances cannot single out a particular employee and treat that employee differently if the employee is part of the bargaining unit.

Because it is difficult to conceive of an employment contract between an employer and a bargaining unit that would not be reduced to writing, and because the negotiation process is not something in which the employee is individually involved, we will focus our discussion on the situations on which an individual employee and employer create a unique contractual relationship. In such situations we would expect to find coaches, athletic directors, and those who work at fitness centers, health clubs, and other such facilities. Often in such individualized situations, the parties fail to create a written contract memorializing the final agreement, and this is even more likely where part-time employment is concerned. The failure to create a written contract can have negative consequences when disagreements arise. Although we've said this before, its repetition here cannot hurt. The elements of a contract, including a personal service contract are as follows:

- meeting of the minds,
- legal subject,
- offer and acceptance,
- consideration,
- legal capacity of parties, and
- precise terms.

In addition to the elements required for an enforceable contract, other good business practices are universal, whether we are talking about a contract for the purchase of goods or a personal service contract. These practices include the following:

- Put it in writing.
- Consider creating a liquidated damages clause in case one party breaches the contract.
- Include all terms of performance that are of significance to either party (such as "time of the essence" or "win/loss record serving as a basis for evaluation").

Even though the elements and related issues of an enforceable contract are consistent regardless of the type of contract, there are issues unique to personal service contracts. Among these issues are the status of the employee, termination and liquidated damages clauses, restrictive covenants, disclosure of outside income clauses, and unique employee behavioral requirements.

Status of the Employee

Many high schools and colleges hire their part-time coaches as "independent contractors"; in an attempt to emphasize that designation (in order to relieve their institutions of the obligation to pay Social Security, withhold taxes, and so forth), a contract is created focusing on the status of the coach rather than including important contractual details. This can lead to negative results when disagreements arise.

The federal government has specific rules about an employer's obligation to pay half of the Social Security taxes of employees (amounting to about 7.5 percent of the total salary). In addition, the employer may need to withhold income taxes, which can become an accounting headache for the employer. Also, the employer may need to pay unemployment and/or workers' compensation insurance premiums for the employee. All these "extras" increase the direct expense of the employer as well as the indirect costs of bookkeeping. Many employers search for a means of circumventing these additional expenses. One method frequently used—but used, in most cases, in violation of the law and its regulations—is to claim that the status of the coach or fitness instructor is that of an independent contractor rather than that of an employee.

Someone who works as an independent contractor remains responsible for such expenses as his or her own taxes and 100 percent of his or her Social Security contributions. The "employer" is not responsible.

On the other hand, someone who works as an employee remains responsible for his or her own taxes but is aided by the employer's obligation to help the employee prepare for paying income taxes by withholding them. The approximately 15 percent of income that must be paid for Social Security taxes is contributed half by the employer and half by the employee.

A comparison under each status for a part-time coach who is earning $2,000 for the season would show that the:

- Independent contractor agrees to work for $2,000 and receives $2,000. Then the independent contractor must pay $300 (15 percent of $2,000) for Social Security plus whatever income taxes may be due.
- Employee agrees to work for $2,000 and receives $1,850 (less whatever income taxes are withheld for application to the

tax bill due) but does not pay any additional amount out of pocket for Social Security taxes.

Therefore, if both the independent contractor and the true employee owe the same total income tax, the independent contractor will have $150 less spendable money. On the other hand, the employee will cost the employer $150 more than will the independent contractor. The independent contractor earns less spendable money, must be careful to save sufficient money to pay income tax, and will not be eligible for such benefits as unemployment insurance. The employee will earn more money, does not need to worry about saving money to pay income tax (assuming sufficient amounts are being withheld), and is eligible in most instances for unemployment insurance and worker's compensation.

The employment status, therefore, is of major significance to both parties to the contract: The worker who accepts the status of an independent contractor loses and the "employer" gains. However, the Internal Revenue Service uses a specific set of criteria to define what is meant by "independent contractor," and part-time coaches simply do not meet the criteria.

The penalties for erroneously designating an employee as an independent contractor are minor at the hands of the IRS, so the practice continues. The penalties for the employee, although more subtle than the $50 fine imposed on the employer, can be great indeed.

Hold harmless laws, which are found in most public educational settings, protect and defend an employee who, while in the furtherance of the employer's interest, is negligent. The concept of hold harmless laws is discussed more fully in Chapters 6 and 14, but it is important to note here in our discussion of independent contractors that the benefits of hold harmless laws are generally denied to independent contractors. Similarly, the doctrine of *respondeat superior*, also discussed at greater length in Chapter 3, which sometimes directs the injured plaintiff's attention at the boss rather than the employee, does not apply to independent contractors. The benefits of both hold harmless laws and the *respondeat superior* doctrine are important and valuable ones that the coach who agrees to be classified as an independent contractor gives up.

Termination Clauses and Liquidated Damages

College and professional coaches often earn a substantial amount of money from sources other than their salaries. Shoe contracts, television appearances, summer camp income, use of cars and country club memberships, and housing benefits add to their incomes in amounts sometimes much greater than their salaries.

If such a coach is terminated before the end of the contract period, does the employing college owe the terminated coach the amount of the perks and outside income that would have been earned absent the firing? Rather than take a chance on the answer to the question at the hands of a jury, both the coach and the college should negotiate the answer at the time the contract is created instead of when the contract is terminated. The negotiation process should include a full discussion of the amounts and types of perks and outside income anticipated and then, from the college's side, the contract should clearly state that the college is not responsible for any compensation other than the salary if the contract should be prematurely terminated without cause. From the coach's side, the negotiations will lean toward including in a liquidated damages clause for the continuation of full salary to the end of the term of the original contract period and compensation for as many of the perks as possible and outside income identified in the negotiation process.

Restrictive Covenants

We have discussed the situation in which the coach is fired, but how can the college protect its interests if the coach breaches the contract by leaving before the end of the contract period? In reality, the college left without a coach is not made whole by having the coach pay liquidated damages. What the college needs is a coach. So the college has two main options it might want to negotiate at the time of creating the original contract.

The first option is, in effect, a legal bribe to encourage the coach to remain throughout the term of the contract. A bonus or base salary increase payable only at the completion of the term of the contract may entice the coach to stay. The second option is a restrictive covenant prohibiting the coach from taking another coaching job in competition with the college. Restrictive covenants, sometimes called "covenants not to compete," are more likely to be enforceable if they are narrowly and reasonably drawn.

Disclosure of outside income clauses and unique employee behavioral requirements such as full compliance with the rules of the National Collegiate Athletic Association, the National Association of Intercollegiate Athletics, and other sports governance associations are increasingly being added to the contracts of an institution's coaches. For instance, recruiting rules are very specific, and their violation by a coach may have severe consequences for the entire institution. The disclosure to the institution or the governance organization of a coach's outside income that is athletically related is required in some instances.

An institution desiring to make it explicitly clear to its coach that it expects the coach to adhere to NCAA rules, for instance, should include a clause in the contract saying so. Putting teeth into such a clause may be done by including a statement that failure to fully adhere to all rules and regulations of the institution as well as the governance organization will be considered a material breach of the contract.

In the negotiation of personal service contracts in general, the wise employer and employee think ahead to what can go wrong with their association with each other and negotiate clauses to protect them from the acts of the other. If it's not in writing, it's not in the contract in a way that is easily enforceable, if enforceable at all.

What Happens When It Doesn't Work Out?

If, without a justifiable cause, an employer fires an employee prior to the end of the contract term, the employer has materially breached the contract and owes the ex-employee damages. If the contract does not include a liquidated damages clause, the ex-employee may have to sue for judicially determined damages.

What are justifiable causes that would allow a coach, teacher, administrator, or fitness leader to be fired prior to the completion of the contract period without placing the employer in the state of breach? There are three main categories of causes of dismissal substantial enough to allow an employer to fire an employee at midterm of the contract without risking successful claims of breach against the employer. The three categories are:

- immorality (e.g., dishonesty in research, theft, lying about a resume, sexual misconduct),

- insubordination (e.g., continually arguing with a supervisor so that the flow of the program is damaged, refusing to attend required faculty meetings, ignoring specific instructions from the chairperson or other administrator), or
- incompetence (e.g., lack of knowledge for the job, failure to exercise sufficient supervision or appropriate teaching methods, placing students at unreasonable physical or psychological risk, or simply not fulfilling the duties of the job in a professional manner).

In addition to falling within one of the "Three I" categories (immorality, insubordination, incompetence), a sufficient reason to dismiss someone at midterm must also have some connection to the job.

The political beliefs, living arrangements, or sexual orientation of an employee, although they might be considered related to the morals of the teacher, coach, or administrator, are generally not a suitable basis for dismissal, even if they are contrary to the views of the community or the boss. Such reasons are not a suitable basis for dismissal because they have no nexus with or connection to the performance of the duties of the job.

On the other hand, reasons for dismissal such as being consistently late to the gymnasium (incompetence because of failure to provide adequate supervision), using a personal car to transport students in contravention to stated school policy (insubordination because of failure to adhere to school policy), or encouraging unhealthy and illegal practices such as the use of anabolic steroids (immorality because of illegality of act encouraged) would provide a sufficient basis for midterm dismissal without placing the employer automatically in a position of breach. In addition to sufficient cause, any midterm firing must also include sufficient due process (the concept of due process is discussed more fully in Chapter 12).

If an employer decides not to rehire an employee at the end of a contract term, no cause needs to exist or, if one does exist, it doesn't need to be articulated. A nonreappointment is not a firing. There is no need to observe due process if an employee is not reappointed. Due process (including an articulation of cause) is owed only when a dismissal occurs before the end of the contract term, unless a specific, and unusual, contract clause requires articulation of the cause of nonreappointment.

Memory Testers

1. True/False. Personal service contracts must be in writing in order to be enforceable.

2. True/False. If you are a marketing agent for a sporting goods manufacturer and you want to make a deal with a 16-year-old Olympic gold medalist to advertise your products, you can successfully bind the minor to the contract by getting both parents to sign the contract.

3. True/False. There are two basketball players named Pat Smith. One is 4 feet tall and clumsy and the other is 7 feet tall and never misses. Over the phone you (a professional basketball coach) make a deal to hire Pat, thinking you are getting the 7-foot Pat, but you are actually talking to the ecstatic-at-the-contract-but-sure you've-made-a-mistake 4-foot Pat. You are obligated to pay 4-foot Pat.

4. Short Answer. What might be appropriate clauses to include in contract negotiations if you were the athletic director hiring a basketball coach for a highly competitive Division I college?

5. Short Answer. What might be appropriate clauses to include in contract negotiations if you were going to be the new coach of a highly competitive Division I basketball team?

6. Short Answer. What are the "Three I's" that represent the three categories of causes sufficient to fire an employee at midterm of the contract?

Memory Tester Discussion

1. False. Contracts involving real property need to be in writing in order to be enforceable, but most other contracts, including personal service contracts, do not generally need to be in writing. However, it is difficult to prove what was agreed upon if a contract is not reduced to writing. Therefore, adopt the rule, "Put it in writing." An interesting case involving prob-

lems arising out of an oral contract for personal service is found in *Rooney v. Michael Tyson*, 91 NY 2d 685, 697 N.E. 2d 571, 674 NYS 2d 616 (1998).

2. False.   Minors can void contracts. The parents of the minor cannot bind the minor. The only way to bind a minor to a contract is to go to court and have a judge approve the contract, thus binding the minor.

3. False.   There was no meeting of the minds, thus there was never any contract to enforce. If 4-foot Pat played for you and later you decided you had made a mistake, 4-foot Pat could sue for wages under the doctrine of *quantum meruit* but could not sue for breach of contract because there never was a contract.

4–6.   See text of Chapter 10.

Related Issues

This chapter is subtitled "Hiring and Firing." There are several more topics to be discussed that relate to, but are not basic to, the understanding of contract law.

Negligent Hiring

If you hire a teacher, Lee, for example, who later molests one of your school's students, are you, as the hiring person, liable to the students who are victimized by Lee? The answer is "No" if you were not negligent in carrying out your duty to hire qualified teachers.

If, on the other hand, you did not do the things a prudent, reasonable, up-to-date administrator would do to check out the qualifications of a potential new teacher, the answer would be, "Yes, you were negligent." The currently used phrase to express this kind of negligence is "negligent hiring." The concept of negligent hiring is just developing in the law, and few cases against administrators have been successfully brought to conclusion. Even though this is a developing area of the law, the prudent administrator would appropriately evaluate potential employees, including a full review of references.

If Lee had previously molested children and a review of Lee's references would have told you that fact, your failure to check the references would be a breach of duty that caused the harm of molestation to your students. All of the required elements of negligence would exist.

Even though negligent hiring is an emerging area of the law, anyone who is responsible for hiring personnel to work with young people should be particularly careful to do all those things that a prudent, reasonable, up-to-date administrator would do to check out the qualifications of a candidate for employment. This does not mean that you hire a private investigator or ask to see the past five years of income tax returns. Instead, being prudent means, within the strictures of maintaining appropriate professional respect for the privacy rights of the prospective employee, you review appropriate materials and interview people who should be interviewed about topics of the candidate's qualifications and behavior relating to potential job performance.

Intentional Interference with a Contractual Right

When an athletic director wants to hire a coach who is currently working at another school, the tort of intentional interference with a contractual right becomes a possibility.

This tort occurs when the following elements exist:

- a contract exists,
- the defendant knew of the contract's existence,
- the defendant intentionally tried to cause the employee to breach the existing contract,
- the employee breaches the original contract, and
- the original employer's interests are damaged by the breach.

If the athletic director enticed a coach currently under contract with another school to leave that school in midterm of the existing contract, and did so knowingly, and the breach injured the original employer, the original employer could sue the athletic director for intentional interference with a contract right. Damages might include the cost of retaining a similarly skilled coach in mid-season, lost revenue from declining gate receipts, and so forth. The original employer could also sue the ex-coach for breach of contract.

It is not intentional interference with a contract right for an athletic director to talk or even negotiate with the coach of another school about creating a contract that would start after the conclusion of the original contract. It only becomes a tort when the athletic director does so with the intent of causing the coach to leave in the midst of the existing contract.

Although not strictly an issue of intentional interference with a contractual right, the recent NCAA restricted earning case involves interesting legal issues relating to contracts. The case, *Law v. NCAA*, Docket Number, U.S. Court of Appeals, Tenth Circuit, 96-3034, 1998, involved the setting of salary caps by the NCAA on the earnings of certain employees, not of the NCAA, but of NCAA member institutions. The case makes interesting reading.

Renegotiation of Contracts

Before we leave the topic of contracts, a parting word about the renegotiation of contracts seems in order. The term "renegotiation" is inaccurate. Once the parties to a contract have committed themselves to the terms of a contract (contract formation), neither party has any legal obligation to do anything other than live up to the provisions of the contract. When a successful professional athlete attempts to renegotiate a contract in midterm by threatening to refuse to play, the legal term that should stand in the place of the frequently but inaccurately used term of "renegotiation" should be "extortion.",

If you were hired to teach a class, it seems obvious that halfway through the semester, you would have no legal standing to go to your department chairperson and demand an increase in salary and, if not granted, threaten to become a less-than-adequate teacher. The same legal concept applies to athletes who attempt to renegotiate at midterm, but somehow society doesn't seem to see it as clearly.

To state the legal principle clearly: Once a contract is created, neither party has any duty to do anything more than live up to the terms of the original contract.

Practice Scenario

Pat and Chris are both hired as coaches at Urban State University. Pat is hired as the volleyball coach as an independent contractor for a total of $42,000 for the year. Chris is hired as the swimming coach as an employee for $40,000.

- Who will have the greatest gross pay for the year's work? Why?
- Who will have the greatest net earnings for the year's work? Why?

- Who is most likely to have the greatest protection from liability if an athlete is injured due to the coach's negligence?
- Whose employment status is incorrect? Why?

How About Looking Up Some Cases?

You might find it interesting to read some of the following cases. Some have value as precedents within their jurisdictions, others don't. So don't assume that the outcome would be the outcome in your jurisdiction. Read them to gain an insight into how the issues of contract law are evaluated. As you read them, develop arguments of your own for the plaintiff and then for the defendant. If you're planning on using the internet, check the Appendix for suggested sites.

Hegener v. Chicago Board of Education, 567 N.E. 2d 566 (Ill. App. I Dist. 1991). This case concerns a school board's decision to dismiss a tenured high school teacher on the basis of irremediable conduct unbecoming a teacher, including inappropriate personal relationships with students.

Law v. NCAA, Docket Number, U.S. Court of Appeals, Tenth Circuit, 96-3034, (1998). This case relates to the restricted earning efforts relating to NCAA member colleges' assistant coaches.

Rodgers v. Georgia Tech Athletic Association, 303 S.E. 2d 467 (Ga. Ct. App. 1983). Pepper Rodgers, after being fired as football coach at Georgia Tech, was paid his remaining two years of salary but sued for the loss of "perks" and other outside income he earned because of his association with the Georgia Tech team.

Rooney v. Michael Tyson, 91 NY 2d 685, 697 N.E. 2d 571, 674 NYS 2d 616 (1998). Boxer Mike Tyson and his trainer litigated a dispute arising out of an oral contract.

Tarkanian v. NCAA, 741 P. 2d 1345 (1987). This high profile case (and its progeny) about a well-known collegiate basketball coach is still in the headlines and the courts.

Chapter 11

Property Rights: "It's Mine"

In a universal sense, rights associated with property and owner-ship include not just land and buildings, or books and furniture, but also the ownership of liberty and life. This chapter will discuss the more tangible items usually considered "property" rather than the "ownership" of life and liberty. Life and liberty rights more logi-cally fall within the context of constitutionally guaranteed rights and so are discussed in Chapter 12.

Rights in Real Property

Landlord/Tenant

If you lease space for a fitness center, you have made a contract which involves real property rights and, more specifically, landlord/tenant relationships.

Landlord/tenant law is a hybrid of two areas of the law: prop-erty and contract. A lease conveys rights in the use of real property

(property law), and it also involves mutual promises or covenants (contract law).

Why does it matter if landlord/tenant controversies are resolved using the principles of contract law versus property law? It matters because it drastically affects the potential outcomes if something goes wrong between the landlord and the tenant.

The promises which are exchanged between landlord and tenant are often considered to be contractual, thus are governed by contract law. On the other hand, a right to possess, use, or own property falls under the tenets of property law. Confused? How about an example:

> You find a perfect location for your new fitness center in the middle of a busy shopping center. The lease/rental agreement you sign with the landlord includes a clause in which the landlord promises not to rent any other space in the shopping center to a fitness center for the duration of your lease. Another clause in the lease/rental agreement includes a promise by the landlord to paint the interior of the space.
>
> The landlord fails to paint the facilities and, worse yet, a month after your center opens, you learn that the landlord has rented the space next door to another fitness center. It is obvious that the shopping center cannot support two fitness centers, so your new business is likely to be ruined. Do you still have the obligation of paying the rent for space which, if you try to do business there, will result in the end of your business? It depends.

The type of law used to deal with landlord/tenant controversies makes a big difference. If you have a problem getting the landlord to honor the painting clause, your dispute more logically fits into the framework of contract law. So, while you must continue to pay rent, you also have the right to sue the landlord for damages based on the breached promise to paint. The promise to paint the premises is thus governed by contract law.

Your use of the fitness center facilities is governed by property law, so as long as you continue to occupy the facilities, you need to pay rent. That doesn't seem quite fair, even if you remember you can sue the landlord for damages. So the courts, in certain circumstances, view the landlord's breach not as only a contract law issue but also as a property law issue.

In our fitness center example, the landlord's breach of contract relating to the neighboring fitness center is so significant that it may equal constructive eviction. If eviction is involved, property law governs. If you, as the fitness center tenant meet the elements below, most jurisdictions will relieve you of the obligation to pay rent. This is a property law, not a contract law, result. In addition, you might be able to sue for damages (such as losses from advertising your grand opening, telephone installation charges, etc.) because of the landlord's breach—a contract law result.

Elements: Constructive Eviction

In order to claim constructive eviction and thereby avail yourself potentially of remedies and relief from obligations under *both* property law and contract law principles, you must be able to show the following three elements:

- **Substantial interference with use and enjoyment of the leased premises.** The interference need have nothing to do with physically occupying the premises. "Substantial" is objectively measured by what a reasonable person would find incompatible with using the premises in the means the parties knew were intended. Courts will take into account factors such as:
  - purpose for which the premises were leased,
  - foreseeability of interference,
  - potential duration of the interference,
  - nature and degree of harm, and
  - methods available to remove interference.

- **Landlord at fault.** The actions of the landlord were significantly involved in causing the interference. If a third party interfered, constructive eviction cannot be claimed unless the landlord encouraged or expressly or impliedly consented to the interference.
- **Tenant moves out.** The tenant must physically move out in order for constructive eviction to be claimed.

Scenario

Contract versus Property Law

Consider the following scenario. Decide if the tenant might be able to claim constructive eviction and thereby gain the ability to use both property law and contract law to find remedies in the courts.

Your school district has scheduled its championship basketball tournament for noon on April 1. You have signed a rental agreement with Urban University to use its gymnasium for the tournament because it includes seating for 2,000. On the morning of April 1, the landlord brings in a painting crew to paint the gym and resurface the gym floor. The gym will not be playable until at least April 4. You make a few frantic calls when you discover the problem and find another school's gym available. You transfer the tournament to the second school but have to pay more rent, increased security fees, and transportation costs. You move all the supplies you had previously delivered to the first gym in anticipation of the tournament. Do you owe rent for the first gym? Can you sue the landlord of the first gym for your extra expenses incurred by having to move the tournament's location?

The relationship between landlord and tenant is often defined by common law principles. For instance, the duties of landlords and tenants are reasonably clear under common law principles.

Duties of the Landlord

The landlord and tenant may decide to add a clause to the lease indicating who has the obligation to make repairs. When there is no clause, the common law of the jurisdiction is applied unless there is specific legislation indicating who should make repairs.

Although residential leases in some jurisdictions, by way of specific legislation, place the obligation to repair on the landlord, in commercial rentals most jurisdictions place the obligation to repair on the tenant. However, even if the tenant has the obligation to repair, the landlord remains liable to people other than the tenant for repairing hidden defects known to the landlord before giving the premises to the tenant, plus hallways, public ways, and other common areas if the landlord retains possession of them.

Landlord's Duties:

- Responsible for making certain repairs
- Guarantee quiet enjoyment of premises

The landlord must guarantee quiet enjoyment of the premises. That doesn't mean that the landlord guarantees the tenant of a good night's sleep or the absence of barking dogs from the next-door neighbor's yard. The covenant of quiet enjoyment means that the landlord will not disrupt the tenant's occupation of the premises by either actual or constructive eviction.

Duties of Tenant

The primary obligation of the tenant is to pay rent. If a tenant fails to pay rent, the landlord can evict the tenant or sue for the missing rent as it accrues.

The landlord is under no obligation to try to

> **Tenant's Duties**
>
> • Pay rent
> • Make vital repairs to prevent decay

find another renter for the remaining term of the lease/rental agreement if the tenant moves out without being evicted. If the landlord evicts the tenant, the obligation to pay rent ceases for any remaining portion of the lease following the eviction.

Unless the law says otherwise or the lease contains a clause to the contrary, common law gives the tenant the responsibility to make repairs which are required to prevent permanent damage to the premises caused by neglect. The tenant does not need to make substantial or lasting repairs but must take those actions which would protect the premises from the elements. Repair obligations in residential rentals often reside with the landlord by statute, but the same is not true of commercial rentals.

The advice to "Put it in writing" is often a requirement when real property is concerned. A confusing doctrine in the law is called the "Statute of Frauds." The Statute of Frauds says, among other things, that contracts which cannot be fulfilled within one year must be in writing to be enforceable by the courts. If you want to rent a storefront for a period of two years for a fitness center, by definition the contract cannot be fulfilled within one year. Therefore, such a contract/lease *must* be in writing to be enforceable. The Statute of Frauds requirement of a written contract also applies when real estate is purchased.

Memory Testers: Landlord/Tenant

1. True/False. Constructive eviction provides the landlord with additional rights.
2. True/False. Anytime a landlord breaches a clause of the lease, the tenant can walk away from the rest of the lease/rental agreement.
3. True/False. A 6-month rental agreement must be in writing in order to be enforceable.

Memory Tester Discussion: Landlord/Tenant

1. False.   Constructive eviction is a doctrine which gives the tenant, not the landlord, a chance of additional options under the law if the landlord has done things which make the continued lease/rental of the premises useless to the tenant. The legal theory which is involved in constructive eviction is property law rather than contract law, thereby potentially relieving the tenant of the obligation to pay rent as well as sue for damages.

2. False.   Most breaches by the landlord only allow the tenant to sue for damages under contract law rather than vacate the premises under the doctrine of constructive eviction in property law.

3. False.   The Statute of Frauds applies to contracts which cannot be completed within a year. However, it is always very good advice to have a written contract, regardless of the length of the rental.

Rental of School Sports Facilities

Many schools rent their sports facilities to outside community groups such as adult education classes, youth groups, or community sports clubs. These rentals are often entered into more as a community service than as a moneymaking endeavor. However, regardless of the motivation for renting facilities to outside groups, the school may be taking on potential liability which it has not contemplated.

School administrative personnel are often not on campus when the community group is using the facilities. Even if school personnel are present, they often assume that supervision of the activity rightly belongs to the renters, not the school. When an injury occurs, all assumptions seem suspect. So if your school or program rents its facilities to community groups, its rental agreement should be either formulated or reviewed by the school attorney. Among the items which need to be considered are:

- Do you want the renters to indemnify the school and its employees from all expenses (including the expense of defending) related to lawsuits arising out of the rental or the use of the rented facilities? If the answer is yes, and it should be, how are you going to accomplish the indemnification? Some schools require the renters to provide a copy of an appropriate insurance policy which indemnifies the school. Are waivers appropriate for the age level?

- What would the prudent school administration do in order to make sure that the renters are supervising the activities appropriately? Would the prudent school require the renters to pay for school personnel to be present or formally agree to an appropriate number and skill level of outside supervisors to be present? (Your choice might be affected by the law in your jurisdiction concerning the school's liability for activities which are at least partially under the control of its personnel.) Would the prudent school require a specific level of supervision by certified staff at areas such as the swimming pool?

- What provisions have been made for the renters to seek emergency medical care if an injury occurs? Is access to a phone provided?

- What provisions should be implemented to require the renters to pay for any damages to the premises?

- Is there a need to have a formal agreement about how much security needs to be present and who pays for the security?

- What provisions should be made to ameliorate the wear and tear placed on the facilities by outside rentals?
- Will the renters or the school be responsible for premises-related injuries? Will the renters or the school be responsible for activity-related injuries?

If your program is buying or selling rather than renting, the advice of an attorney should always be sought. It is beyond the scope of this book to discuss the legal principles of buying and selling real property.

Rights in Creative Property

This book carries a copyright. I, the author, wrote the book and then placed a copyright restriction on it so that the manuscript could not be copied without my permission for a period of my lifespan plus 70 years. I transferred my copyright to the publisher so that the publisher could legally print multiple copies of the book and sell one to you. Thanks.

If you decide to make copies of the book for a friend so that your friend can have one without buying one (you'd better not!) without obtaining the permission of the current holder of the copyright, you will be violating the U.S. Copyright Act, 17 U.S. C. sections 101-810 and I will be very disappointed in you.

My right to control what words appear in this book is derived from the 1st Amendment to the Constitution, often referred to as the Freedom of Speech Amendment.

The right to control the future of those words involves a two-step derivation. First, Article I Section 8 of the Constitution gave Congress, not the individual state legislatures, the power to "Promote the Progress of Science and useful Arts by securing for limited Times to Authors . . . the exclusive Right to their Writings."

Second, Congress has exercised that power by passing several generations of the Copyright Act. The Copyright Act sets out the specific steps authors must follow in order to be able to control the future of their words. The Act also tells those who would like to copy the author's words how they might do so without violating the author's right to control the words in the future.

Even though Congress has written and rewritten copyright legislation for two centuries, confusion remains. In fact, confusion may be increasing due to new technology for disseminating words via the internet and other electronic media plus new legal provisions such as the Doctrine of Fair Use, which is found for the first time in the 1975 version of the law.

What Can Be Copyrighted?

Books and articles are what most people think of when they think about copyrightable materials. However, dance choreographies which have been the subject of notation, fitness software programs, musical compositions, videotaped lectures, rules for a new game, graphic designs, and logos for an athletic program are also copyrightable. In fact, any author's or creator's original work which has been fixed in a tangible form of expression is copyrightable.

What Cannot Be Copyrighted?

Facts cannot be copyrighted. An author of a *Research Quarterly for Exercise and Sport* article cannot copyright the facts discovered. However, the author can copyright the expression of facts. In practice this means that the way the *RQES* author discusses, expresses, or phrases the explanation of the facts discovered is copyrightable, but not the facts themselves. A fact simply exists; no one is the author of a fact.[1]

Ideas cannot be copyrighted. If an author of a *JOPERD* article discusses an idea about the best way to ensure quality physical education for the nation's schoolchildren, the idea is not copyrightable, even though the words used to express it may be.

Separating what is a noncopyrightable fact or idea from what is a copyrightable expression of a fact or idea is difficult. The appearance of the fact or idea within the context of a copyrighted article does not provide assistance, because a noncopyrightable fact or idea can, and often does, appear within a copyrightable article.

The courts have not been uniform in their interpretation of the Copyright Law, and an author who is setting out to use the facts or

---

[1] A bill currently in Congress (December, 1999) contains provisions to allow facts to be copyrighted. This proposal appears to run totally counter to the spirit of copyright principles and would place devastating restrictions on academic research as well as commercial enterprise.

ideas of another without attribution should move cautiously and also consider the ethical ramifications.

How Can a Copyright Be Obtained?

Under the Copyright Law, the creator's creation gains copyright protection as soon as it is created. Let's take a look at the creation of an article. There is no requirement to have the article published, nor is there a requirement to have the article registered with the Copyright Office. But once the article is published or leaves the physical control of the author (for instance if the author lends a copy to a colleague), a notice of copyright should be placed on the article. In general, the notice is simple. The author should include on the article:

1. the symbol ©, the word "Copyright," or the abbreviation "Copr.,"
2. the year of first publication, and
3. the name of the owner of the copyright, for example © Carpenter 2000.

A copyright may also be registered with the Copyright Office, although such registration is not necessary. However, registration is required if the author plans to sue if someone were to copy the article without permission. Registration, if made prior to a copyright infringement, carries with it the advantage of qualifying the copyright owner for a court award of statutory damages and attorney's fees rather than merely damages.

Fair Use Doctrine

There are many areas of the Copyright Law which are in flux, and there are many details of the settled law which are of little current significance to understanding the overall concept of copyrights. However, the Fair Use Doctrine is an area which bears significance as we get ready to push the "Copy" button on the office copying machine.

Prior to the development of the Fair Use Doctrine, most of the copies teachers and coaches made for their students and colleagues were made illegally. The Fair Use Doctrine has enlarged the items which can be copied legally, yet many people still fail to live within its requirements. Consider, for instance, a teacher who, without permission, duplicates chapters found in a number of textbooks so that they can be compiled into an anthology and sold to the students. Is it likely that such a use would be considered "fair" to the authors' copyrights?

There are four factors to be evaluated in determining if the Fair Use Doctrine is being followed:

- **Purpose of use—commercial or educational.** The Fair Use Doctrine only applies to educational purposes.
- **Amount of the overall work to be copied.** Only small portions of a larger work may be copied.
- **Nature of the material to be copied.** Workbooks and consumable materials such as score sheets cannot be copied under the Fair Use Doctrine.
- **Potential effect on the market value of the copyrighted work.** If the duplication results in the loss of a sale of a copy, the market is being altered.

In addition to the four somewhat subjective factors noted above, the Fair Use Doctrine includes 10 specific guidelines for legally making multiple copies for educational use:

1. The copying involves no charge to the students beyond the actual cost.
2. The decision to use the work must be too close to the time of use to obtain permission from the copyright holder.
3. The copying of a particular item is *not* repeated from term to term.
4. The copying is *not* done from works which were intended to be consumable such as workbooks.
5. The copying is *not* being done as a substitute for purchasing books or reprints.
6. Each copy must include a notice of copyright.
7. The copying must be done by or for a teacher at the teacher's individual request rather than directed by a higher authority.
8. The copying is for only one course in the school.
9. Not more than one article (story, short poem, essay, or two excerpts) from the same author nor more than three from the same collective work during one class term may be copied.

10. The use of multiple copying comprises nine or fewer instances during one class term.

Although lawsuits based on copyright infringement are few in the educational area, they do occur. The cost of defending against such a lawsuit is not covered by insurance or hold harmless laws.

Risk Management and Property Rights

The single most important risk management technique is one which is proactive rather than reactive: Get it in writing! Whether it is a lease or a promise to paint a rented space or an agreement about who should provide lifeguards when an outside group rents your pool, you should make sure the agreement is in writing.

The more significant the problems which would result from a dispute about property rights might be, the more important it is for you to think ahead. Consider all the possible problems and decide how you want them resolved. Then put it in writing. Negotiate appropriate clauses in lease/rental agreements and copyright those things which you care about not having someone else copy.

If your school or program has developed a logo or mascot image which you plan to license or which would result in financial loss to your program if someone, without your permission, sold copies, get it copyrighted or trademarked, whichever is appropriate for your particular situation.

When your finger gets near a copying machine's "copy" button, review the Fair Use Doctrine requirements and make sure your copying will comply *or* take the time to obtain the copyright holder's permission. Most nonpublisher copyright holders in academe give permission easily. Do the right thing, even if you know it is likely you won't get caught if you were to violate someone's copyright.

How About Reading a Few Cases, and Laws?

Basic Books v. Kinko's Graphics Corp., 758 F. Supp. 1522, 1532 (S.D.N.Y. 1991). This case discusses the importance of a commercial use of copied materials, such as anthologies used as college texts.

llinois High School Association v. GTE Vantage. 99 F. 3d 244 (7th Cir. 1996), cert denied, 519 U.S. 1150, 117 S.Ct 1083 (1997). This case deals with a dispute over who has the right to use the "March Madness" trademark.

Princeton Univ. Press v. Michigan Document Servs., Inc., 99 F 3d 1381 (6th Cir. 1996). This case discusses the impact of commercial use versus Fair Use.

U.S. Copyright Act, 17 U.S.C. sections 101-810. This is the location of the copyright act which has been modified several times. Be sure to also look for the amendments.

Chapter 12
Constitutional Protections: "I Have My Rights"

In the early days of our country, opinions were strong about whether laws and power should be concentrated in the national/federal government or within each state. A republic was the format that allowed a compromise.

In our republic, the states have given certain powers to the federal government but have kept everything else. The U.S. Constitution is a compilation of the powers the states decided were better administered by a national government. For instance, the U.S. Constitution includes the power of the federal government to create an army, print money, and sign treaties. If each state had retained such powers, our foreign and economic policies would be very confusing.

In addition to giving power to the federal government to do things, the U.S. Constitution includes a number of promises, in the form of amendments, made on behalf of the federal government not to do other things. For instance, the 1st amendment guarantees that the federal government will not interfere with our right to speak freely and our freedom to maintain the religious beliefs of our choice.

The 4th Amendment guarantees our right to privacy, including the right to be free from being searched. The 5th Amendment guarantees us due process and a right not to testify against ourselves in criminal matters. Due process means that "fair procedures" must be used before we can be deprived of life, liberty, or property.

If we read the Bill of Rights (the first ten amendments) carefully, we will see that the federal government, and only the federal government, promises to honor these rights. Without something else, the state governments could search us or ban what we say. However, thanks to the 14th Amendment, passed soon after the Civil War, the states, in effect, have added their promises to those of the federal government to protect our rights. The 14th Amendment also gives us something else of great value. It promises that neither the states nor the federal government can treat us unequally (this is often referred to as the Equal Protection Clause).

We will talk later about how some of these specific promises (amendments) relate to sport situations, but first let's talk about the promises made in the U.S. Constitution in general. It is important to understand how the promises work because the same process applies to all of the amendments. Once you understand how to evaluate a constitutional right, you can apply that evaluation process to everything from whether you can order your players to take a drug test to whether denial of your promotion violates one of your constitutional rights.

Evaluation Process Step 1: Is a State Actor Involved?

The only actors that promised us anything in the Constitution are the federal and state governments. The federal and state governments, and any subunit of them, are considered "state actors." The first question in the evaluation process, "Is a state actor involved?" is vitally important because if no state actor is involved, there is no protection promised us, and our progress through the remaining evaluation process would be futile.

Over the years, the Constitution has been interpreted to include promises made not just by the federal and state governments, but by any group that acts in a governmental way. The "governmental way" idea is confusing, but let's try to define it by listing some groups that are consistently considered to be acting in a governmental way and thereby are state actors. On that list would be public school districts, city and county governments, police departments, and municipal recreation departments.

We also know that some groups are definitely not state actors. Included on the "nonstate actor" list would be private fitness programs, diet salons, health spas, and proprietary cardiac rehabilitation centers.

Some groups are state actors and are thus bound whereas others are nonstate actors and are not bound by the promises in the Constitution. But there still remain other groups whose status is uncertain. For instance, is the National Collegiate Athletic Association a state actor and thus bound to honor the promises of the Constitution?

If you were a student athlete who believed the NCAA's drug testing program violated your 4th Amendment right against being searched (a drug test constitutes a search), you would first need to find logical arguments to support the notion that the NCAA is a state actor. This would be necessary because only state actors must honor constitutional rights. Let's begin your argument in support of the notion that the NCAA is a state actor by noting that:

1. The majority of NCAA membership is made up of public colleges and universities, which are state actors themselves.
2. The NCAA functions in a regulatory, "governmental way" as it administers college sports.
3. Drug testing is more of a governmental than a private function.

Can you think of more arguments?

On the other hand, if you were the NCAA and you wanted to support your drug testing program, you would need to develop arguments to support the notion that the NCAA was not a state actor and thus not bound to honor the constitutional right against searches. Try to build an argument supporting the notion that the NCAA is not a state actor.

The truth is that we are not yet certain whether, for drug testing purposes, the NCAA will be determined to be a state actor or not. Some lawsuits involving the NCAA on unrelated, yet constitutional issues have decided the NCAA is a state actor, and many others have decided that the NCAA is not a state actor.

The decision whether an entity is a state actor is all-important, because only state actors have an obligation to protect our constitutional rights. So, for instance, if you work for a nonstate actor, such as a private beach club or fitness center, the club or center can insist on a drug test, and your employer can search your locker without violating your constitutional rights. Of course there may be state laws prohibiting such actions, but at the moment we are only considering U.S. Constitutional law.

Evaluation Process Step 2: How Important Is the Right Being Violated, and How Important Is the Reason for Violating It?

If we determine that the person or group violating our rights is a state actor, then we proceed to step 2 in our evaluation. In step 2 we review the importance of the right being violated.

For the sake of simplicity, our discussion so far has sounded as though our constitutional rights cannot be violated by a state actor with impunity. It is time to become a little more complex in our conceptualization. In reality, any *nonstate* actor can violate our rights all they want in the absence of specific laws to the contrary. Additionally, a *state actor* can violate our rights if, but only if, the state actor has a good enough reason. How good the reason has to be depends on the type of right being violated. In other words, is the right being violated a fundamental right or a nonfundamental right? A nonfundamental right requires only a mild level of scrutiny, whereas the violation of a fundamental right requires a higher, stricter level of scrutiny.

Nonfundamental rights
Lower standard (mild scrutiny):
Rationally related to a **legitimate** state interest

Fundamental rights
Higher standard (strict scrutiny):
Necessary to accomplish a **compelling** state interest

Any state actor that undertakes to violate a nonfundamental constitutional right must be able to show that the reason for doing so is rationally related to a legitimate state interest. If the state actor can show such a reason, that party can proceed with impunity. For example, assume a school prohibits the wearing of earrings during physical education classes. Students might argue that the school is infringing on the students' right to dress as they wish. The reason the school might use to show that the prohibition is okay could be:

The argument:

Rationally related:	Earrings can cut fellow students and can get caught in nets or clothing, thus injuring the wearer. Prohibiting earrings is a **rational** method of preventing such injuries.
Legitimate state interest:	Preventing injuries among its students is a **legitimate** interest of the school (in its role as a state actor).

Does the argument seem reasonable? Probably.

However, any state actor that undertakes to violate a **fundamental** constitutional right must be able to show a more substantial reason for doing so. The state actor must be able to show that the reason for violation and the method of violation is **necessary to accomplish a compelling state interest**. Assume a school requires students to recite a particular prayer at the beginning of each athletic practice and competition. Students might argue that the school is infringing on the students' right to be free from state-imposed religious behavior, a fundamental right (a violation of the 1st Amendment). The school would have to find a sufficiently impressive reason in order to meet the level of scrutiny required for a violation of a fundamental right: that it is necessary to accomplish a compelling state interest. It is difficult to comprehend that the school could find such a reason. The school might argue the following:

The argument:

Necessary:	Recitation of the prayer is the least intrusive, most effective method of accomplishing the school's goal.
Compelling state interest:	Increasing the students' sense of religious identity and thus fostering more disciplined

behavior on their part is a compelling state
interest similar in level to preventing airplanes
from being bombed by searching potential
passengers or preventing someone from cry-
ing "fire!" in a crowded theater.

Does the argument seem reasonable? Probably not.

So we must decide whether the right is a nonfundamental right
or a fundamental right. There is no list of fundamental rights delin-
eated in the Constitution. Instead, the U.S. Supreme Court, through
its series of decisions (case law), has identified a few rights as being
fundamental. For instance, the right to free speech is a fundamental
right. Also among our fundamental rights are the right to be free
from warrantless searches and the right against self-incrimination.

Let's return to our discussion of the drug testing problem. If we
determine that the NCAA is a state actor, then we need to decide
what type of right (fundamental/nonfundamental) a drug test
would violate.

The 4th Amendment right to be free from warrantless searches
and the 5th Amendment right against self-incrimination (the results
of a urine test for illegal drugs is "testimony") are both fundamental
rights. Because a drug test would violate the 4th and 5th Amendment fundamental rights, the NCAA would have to demonstrate a
more substantial reason for conducting its test than simply that the
test is "rationally related to a legitimate state interest."

The NCAA would have to meet the higher standard of being
"necessary to accomplish a compelling state interest." What might
be the compelling state interest served if the NCAA administered
drug tests to athletes? Try to add arguments to this brief list:

• The state has an interest in a drug free citizenry.
• Drug abuse is a problem that goes to the core of the future of
  our country.
• Athletes serve as role models for their peers.
• Keeping athletes drug free helps society at large become more
  drug free.

Assuming you have convinced yourself that the NCAA has a
compelling state interest in conducting drug tests, the second half
of the reasoning must also be met: the means must be necessary. Is
random drug testing necessary? That is, is the testing program the

least restrictive, least invasive, and most efficient method of accomplishing the compelling state interest?

This time try to argue against the necessity of a testing program. For instance:

- There are many false-positives in the drug tests.
- A urine collection in the presence of another is invasive of personal privacy.
- Is there, in fact, data to support the notion that drugs are widely used by athletes?

Can you think of other arguments to support the notion that the drug test used is not the least restrictive and most efficient means of accomplishing the goal?

INTERIM REVIEW

Evaluation of a Claim of Violation of Rights

Step 1: Is a state actor involved, and if "yes," then
Step 2: What type of right is being violated, and is the right being violated for a sufficient reason?

Ordinary, nonfundamental right requires:
- rationally related to a legitimate state interest

Fundamental right requires:
- necessary to accomplish a compelling state interest

Now that you have practiced arguing both sides of the issue, let's review what has to be shown by someone who is claiming that constitutional rights are being unjustly violated.

Practice Scenarios: Constitutional Rights

Evaluate both of the following scenarios and develop arguments for and against constitutionality.

- Four athletes each shave their heads, leaving hair in the form of a different letter of the alphabet on the head of each student. When the four students stand in the correct order, the heads spell out a four-letter word they are planning to show to the rival team. The school's coach and principal learn of the plans and schedule an interview with the students and their attorneys. After the formal interview, the principal and coach decide that the students must either shave the rest of their hair or wear a cap if they wish to play in the game. What issues would need to be considered in order to decide if this action is constitutional?

- An athlete's wallet is stolen at practice. The coach decides to (a) search the lockers of all team members, (b) search the book bags of all team members, and (c) conduct body searches of all team members. Are any or all of these searches constitutional?

Due Process and Equal Protection

The Constitution's due process and equal protection clauses involve extra steps in their analyses.

Due Process

The 5th and 14th Amendments both promise that no life, liberty, or property interest can be terminated without due process. "Due process" means that "fair procedures" will be used.

A few examples will help illustrate what is meant by life, liberty, and property interests. Capital punishment obviously deprives someone of their interest in life. The 5th and 14th Amendments guarantee that no state actor can deprive us of our lives without due process, or in other words, fair procedures. A less extreme example would be if, without fair procedures, a state actor barred a college professor from teaching anywhere in the state. The professor's liberty interest in seeking employment elsewhere in the state would be lost by the ban.

Of the three interests (life, liberty, and property) protected by the due process clauses, the interest most frequently involved in sports-related due process cases is a property interest. We have a property interest in our jobs. An athlete has a property interest in a scholarship and an education. None of these interests may be terminated by a state actor without some level of due process.

But what process is due? The more important and substantial our interest is, the more we can expect fair procedures and the more levels of appeal will exist within that fair process. Let's consider the example of Pat, who is a physical education teacher.

- *Pat has a one-year contract. At the end of the year, Pat is not reappointed.* Pat's property interest in the next year's job is slight, thus little or no procedural fairness is owed to Pat.

- *Pat has a one-year contract. Pat is fired after six months.* Unlike the first scenario, Pat has a rather substantial property interest in the last six months of the job. Someone who is in the midst of a contract period has a strong expectation that the job will continue through its term. That expectation cannot be denied without due process. In this specific situation, due process would most likely require Pat's employer to at least (a) identify specifically, significant deficiencies generally found under one of the "Three I" categories of immorality, insubordination, and incompetence, or (b) warn or notify Pat of deficiencies and give Pat an opportunity to rebut or repent.

- *Pat has tenure. Pat is fired.* A tenured teacher has a great expectation of the continuation of employment. Greatly expanded procedural safeguards beyond those listed in the second scenario would have to be used to meet the elevated requirements of due process. Hearings, with Pat having the right to have an attorney present, would be among the expanded procedures. Also, appeal procedures no doubt would be required as well as full documentation of significant errors by Pat in one or more of the "Three I" categories.

Does a hearing mandated by the conventions of due process have to be completed before terminating a property interest such as a job? Not always. It is important to remember that lack of due process can be justified in some instances in much the same manner that other rights can be violated—if the reason is good enough. For instance, if a tenured teacher has adopted the active behavior of an arsonist, bomber, child abuser, or other extremely dangerous person, the teacher can be removed first and hearings can be held after the fact. Certainly in such instances, the protection of the lives of students is a compelling state interest, and the immediate removal of the dangerous teacher may be the least restrictive and most effective necessary method of accomplishing that state interest. However, the obligation of providing an appropriate hearing and other due process requirements after the removal is not lessened.

INTERIM REVIEW: Due Process

When considering a claim of lack of due process, evaluate the claim using the following steps:

Step 1: Is a state actor involved, and if "yes," then

Step 2: Is an interest in life, liberty, or property being infringed, and if "yes," then

Step 3: How significant is that interest, thus what level of fair procedures is required?

Step 4: If the procedures were insufficient compared to the intensity of the interest involved, is there a sufficient reason for violating the right to due process?

Practice Scenarios: Due Process

Evaluate each of the following scenarios and develop arguments on both sides.

• Chris, a college senior on an athletic scholarship, is hoping for a lucrative professional sports career. Chris is late to practice for the third time in a row, so the coach benches Chris for the week's big game at which professional scouts will be looking for recruits. What interest is being deprived, and what due process requirements might need to be met?

• Jay is a student teacher in the local junior high school. Jay is angered by the constant criticism received from the master teacher, so Jay walks out on the gymnastics class that is supposed to be taught that day by Jay. The master teacher calls the college's student teaching coordinator saying that Jay's actions were insubordinate. Jay thus fails the student teaching course and cannot graduate and cannot get a job. Evaluate this scenario using the steps discussed in this chapter.

Equal Protection

The 14th Amendment guarantees that state actors will treat all of us equally and that we will receive "equal protection under the law." This means that we can't be classified and then treated differently based on our membership in a particular category or class. Anytime a state actor treats a class or category of people differently from individuals not in that class, the state actor must be able to show that the disparity of treatment is rationally related to a legitimate state interest. Yes, you remembered correctly; the test of rationally related to a legitimate state interest is the same as the test for violating any ordinary (nonfundamental) right found in the Bill of Rights.

Let's consider the following example. The city recreation department categorizes potential lifeguards according to age and certification. The city recreation department (state actor) then treats the potential lifeguards differently because it will only hire those who are over, let's say, 18 and certified. Is this a violation of the Equal Protection Clause? Yes, but it is permissible if the recreation department can show that its discrimination by age and certification status is rationally related to a legitimate state interest. Can you think of arguments the city recreation department might use in support of its actions? Perhaps the department might argue the following:

1. The maintenance of safe beaches and swimming pools is a **legitimate interest** of the state.

2. The imposition of minimum age and certification requirements is **rationally related** to keeping the city's beaches and swimming pools safe.

In fact, it is quite easy to meet the test of rationally related to a legitimate state interest. If we look at our daily lives we will find we are frequently, and constitutionally, categorized and then treated differently based on the classification we fall into.

However, some forms of classification are suspicious. These suspect classifications are based on the "RAN" classifications of:

- Race,
- Alienage (e.g., grandparents were Irish), and
- National origin (e.g., born in Ireland).

If one of these three suspect classifications is used as the basis for disparate treatment by a state actor, the state actor must justify the disparate treatment by using a more rigorous standard than merely showing that its actions are rationally related to a legitimate state interest. In fact, the same test used when a fundamental right is violated is used to evaluate categorizations based on one of the RAN classifications.

So disparate treatment by a state actor based on race, alienage, or national origin is only permissible if it is necessary to accomplish a compelling state interest.

INTERIM REVIEW: Equal Protection

When considering a claim of violation of the right to equal protection, evaluate the claim using the following steps:

Step 1: Is a state actor involved, and if "yes," then

Step 2: Is the classification the basis of disparate treatment?

Step 3: What is the basis for classification?

a. If a nonsuspect classification is used, can the state actor successfully claim that the classification is rationally related to a legitimate state interest?

b. If a suspect classification (RAN) is used, can the state actor successfully claim that the disparate treatment is necessary to accomplish a compelling state interest?

Race, alienage and nationality, called suspect classifications, are the three types of classifications which require strict scrutiny when they are used to discriminate. Gender and disability are not currently considered suspect classifications. However, several U.S. Supreme Court decisions have indicated that gender and disability-based classifications must be justified by something more than the rationally related to a legitimate state interest test yet less than necessary to accomplish a compelling state interest which would be applied to the suspect classifications of race, alienage, or national origin.

So at present, there seems to be a developing mid-level test or scrutiny. The development by the Supreme Court of this apparent mid-level test for gender and disability-based classifications seems to be indicative of a growing concern and sensitivity about discrimination based on either gender or disability. Indeed, Congress has enacted specific legislation concerning both gender discrimination, such as Title IX, and disability, such as the Americans with Disabilities Act (ADA). (Title IX and the ADA are discussed more fully in Chapter 13.)

The constitutional analysis used when someone claims that a constitutional right has been violated involves the question: "Did they have a good reason?" On the other hand, when someone is accused of violating the provisions of legislation, such as Title IX or the ADA, the analytic process is somewhat more objective: "Did they do it?" So although discrimination can be attacked using constitutional analyses, it can also be attacked using an entirely different process and analysis, through legislation such as Title IX and the ADA.

Practice Scenarios: Equal Protection

- The school board of Local High School has decided to raise the academic standards of intramural sports participants so that the students will be more aware of the importance of good study habits. The new rule says that in order to participate on a team sport, a player must maintain a B grade point average (GPA), and in order to participate in an individual sport, a player must maintain a B+ GPA. No participation is allowed if the minimum GPA is not met. Is this proposal constitutional? Consider all the constitutional issues.

- Coach Chris can only have 10 members on the swimming team. Coach Chris uses scores on five different swimming skill tests plus racing times in three strokes to determine team membership. Half of the 20 applicants are excluded from the team. Is this constitutional? Consider all the constitutional issues.

- The NCAA drug testing program is administered only to athletes. The rest of the student body is not tested. On this issue alone, what constitutional issues should be considered?

We have been talking about techniques of constitutional analysis and the general constitutional protections found in the 5th and 14th Amendments. The analysis of constitutional protections is the same regardless of the source of the right, but it might be a good idea to briefly review some of the amendments and the rights they convey.

1st Amendment. The 1st Amendment provides protections relating most generally to speech, including symbolic speech and religion, including pregame prayers. The protections found in the 1st amendment are of a fundamental nature and thus are generally reviewed using strict scrutiny. The prohibition of hate speech, a current topic of discussion, is an issue which would be reviewed using the principles of the 1st Amendment. The underpinnings of defamation also stem from the 1st amendment.

4th Amendment. The 4th Amendment provides protections relating most generally to searches. Long considered a fundamental right, the right to be free from warrantless searches has been somewhat eroded by the Supreme Court's *Vernonia* decision. The courts have been contending with issues of individualized suspicion versus random searches and their acceptability within the framework of the 4th Amendment. School violence and drug use have been the two main behavioral factors which have seemed to result in some people's desire to erode 4th Amendment protections for students. However, the courts are still struggling with the issue, so this topic is an interesting one to watch unfold.

5th Amendment. The 5th Amendment includes portions of the due process protections which, for instance, relate to expelling or suspending students. The 5th Amendment also relates to protections from self-incrimination which is playing a role in the evaluation of the constitutionality of drug testing on campus.

8th Amendment. Although it has not found success as a bar to corporal punishment, the 8th Amendment has been employed in the fight against corporal punishment.

11th Amendment. The 11th Amendment relates to state immunity from lawsuits based in federal law. It seems very far afield from any application to schools, physical education, or sport programs. However, there are several cases currently at the Supreme Court which are using the 11th Amendment, and its historic relationship to Article 3 of the Constitution, to argue that federal legislation such as Title VII (anti-discrimination in the workplace), ADA (anti-discrimination based on disability) and Title IX (anti-discrimination in schools based on gender) should not be applicable to state institutions such as state colleges and universities. If the Supreme

Court interprets the issues to bar the application of federal laws such as those noted above to state institutions, there will certainly be big headlines, so you won't miss it. This is an extremely significant area of the law to watch.

14th Amendment.   The 14th Amendment includes additional issues relating to due process, but its main claim to fame derives from its Equal Protection Clause. If the 11th Amendment issues currently at the Supreme Court (and discussed above) result in the barring of civil rights lawsuits against state institutions, the 14th amendment will need to be more heavily relied upon in the area of civil rights.

Risk Management Regarding Constitutional Issues

There is no coverage through insurance or hold harmless laws for someone who violates another's constitutional rights. Some insurance policies at least protect the defendant who is later found by the courts to be not guilty from having to pay attorney's fees for the successful defense. However, the risk managment technique is to understand the basic constitutional guarantees and analysis techniques and adhere to them.

How About Looking Up a Few Cases?

If you're near a law library, you might find it interesting to read some of the following cases. Some have value as precedents within their jurisdictions, others don't. So don't assume that the outcome would be the outcome in your jurisdiction. However, read them to gain an insight into how the issues of constitutional protection are evaluated. As you read them, develop arguments of your own for the plaintiff and then for the defendant. If you plan on using the internet to find cases, check the Appendix for suggested sites.

> *Goss v. Lopez*, 419 U.S. 565 (1975). Suspension of students raises constitutional issues. *Goss* provides the classic and controlling view of the issues.

> *Hysaw v. Washburn University*, 690 F. Supp. 940 (1987). This case discusses the property rights players have or don't have in collegiate athletics and 1st Amendment rights.

Menora v. Illinois High School Association, 527 F. Supp. 637 (1981). This case involves constitutional issues concerning basketball headgear.

New Jersey v. TLO, 105 S.Ct. (1985). This is a classic case that changed the way we view the obligations incurred when a school official wants to search a student's locker.

San Francisco Arts & Athletics, Inc. et al. v. United States Olympic Committee, et al, 483 US 22 (1987). Does the USOC's blocking the use of the word "Olympic" by a gay group organizing an athletic competition violate the group's 1st Amendment rights? This case includes some interesting discussions and, in addition, is informative about the USOC's relationship with the federal government.

Vernonia School District 47J v. Acton et ux., Guardians ad Litem for Acton. 115 S.Ct. 2386 (1995). This 5–4 opinion provides very interesting reading about the use of drug testing for high school athletes.

Race to Constitutionality

The diagram on the opposite page is a memory tickler designed to help you remember the various hurdles (levels of scrutiny) over which a state actor must jump in order to violate various constitutional rights. Follow the race, step by step, to determine which path a particular contestant/violator must travel. Also note that the courts have made an intermediate, ill-defined path, calling for greater scrutiny than the low hurdles but less than the high hurdles. The intermediate path is an area of developing law and currently includes discrimination on the basis of gender, age, and disability. However, because the intermediate level is in flux, it is not represented on the diagram.

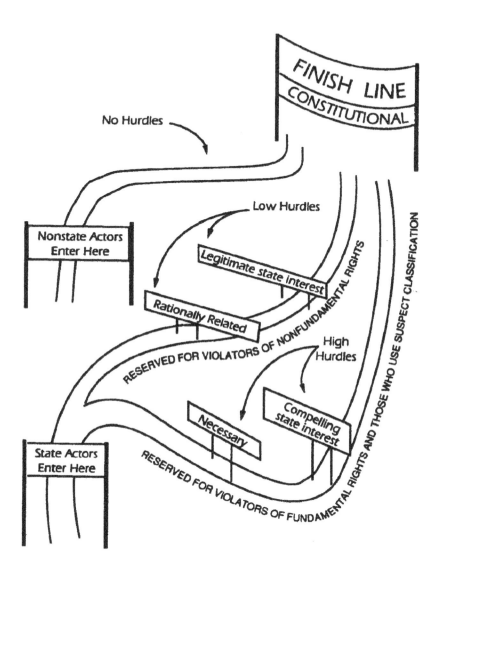

Chapter 13

Legal Concepts of Equity and Equality: "It's Not Fair!"

The U.S. Constitution provides for the equal treatment of us all, absent the showing of a good reason to treat us differently. The equal protection clause of the 14th Amendment is often used by plaintiffs who believe they have been discriminated against unfairly. In addition to the 14th Amendment to the Constitution, there are other laws which also protect us from discrimination. So someone who believes discrimination has occurred can look both to constitutional imperatives as well as statutory imperatives for equity.

Constitutional Imperatives for Equity

The notion that we should all be treated the same under the law has existed, at least theoretically, since the 1868 ratification of the 14th Amendment but in practice has existed for some individuals and groups only after lengthy legal struggles in the courts. The 14th Amendment is five sections long, but the section dealing with equal protection under the law is the first. It reads: "All persons born or naturalized in the United States, and subject to the jurisdiction thereof, are citizens of the United States and of the state wherein they reside. No state shall make or enforce any law which shall abridge the privileges or immunities of citizens of the United States; nor shall any state deprive any person of life, liberty, or property, without due process of law, *nor deny to any person within its jurisdiction the equal protection of the laws.*" [italics added]

These few lines have been interpreted by the Supreme Court to mean, among other important things, that

- The rights found in the Amendments to the Constitution that preceded the 14th, which were to be held inviolate (absent sufficient reason) by the federal government would now also need to be held inviolate by the states and, by extension, local governmental entities as well.

- The citizenship of those individuals who had previously been enslaved was made clear.

- No individual (citizen and noncitizen alike) within the jurisdiction of the various states can lawfully be treated by the states differently from any other person.

The language of the 14th Amendment is difficult to understand, but as we focus on the equal protection clause we'll try to make it clear.

To be considered constitutional, an act by a state that involves disparate treatment based on membership in a particular classification group will need to meet one of the two levels of tests characteristically applied to other constitutionally guaranteed rights. If the category of classification is not one of the suspect classes (or the mid-level areas such as gender and handicapping condition), the level of review applied is determined solely by what right is being violated.

Let's look at a facetious but useful example. Assume that a state legislature passed a statute saying that no one over 6 feet tall would be allowed to attend any state-supported university. Classified as being "vertically enhanced" (tall) is not a suspect classification, nor is it a mid-level classification. Therefore, the courts would generally apply the "rationally related to a legitimate state interest" test to determine the statute's constitutionality. However, if the specific right being denied on the basis of the classification happened to be a fundamental right, then the higher standard of "necessary to accomplish a compelling state interest" would be used. Thus we would need to ask if attending a state university is a fundamental right. The answer is, "No, education of any sort is not a fundamental right." Therefore, the lower standard would be used in our scenario.

Statutory Imperatives for Equity

The Congress of the United States has enacted a number of laws that provide for fair and equal treatment. These laws are in addition to whatever protections are available under the Constitution. These laws are enacted by the Congress, interpreted by the federal judiciary, and enforced by the executive branch (usually in the identity of the Department of Justice).

Title IX of the Education Amendments of 1972,[1] Title VII of the Civil Rights Act of 1964,[2] the Equal Pay Act,[3] the Americans with Disabilities Act (ADA),[4] and Section 504 of the Rehabilitation Act of 1973[5] are among the many equity statutes that have an impact on physical education, sport, and athletics programs. Title IX has had the lion's share of the publicity, and we'll use it as a template for the others.

Title IX

Title IX of the Education Amendments of 1972 says: "No person in the United States shall, on the basis of sex, be excluded from participation in, be denied the benefits of, or be subjected to discrimination under any education program or activity receiving Federal financial assistance."

---

[1] 20 USC sections 1681-87 (1988) as amended by the Civil Rights Restoration Act of 1987, Pub. L. No. 100-259, 102 Stat. 28 (1988) (codified USC section 1687).

[2] 42 USC sections 2000c-2000e-17, plus additions made by the Civil Rights Act of 1991, Pub. L. No. 102-166, 105 Stat 1071 (1991).

[3] 29 CFR Section 1620.

[4] Public Law 101-336, 2 USA, Sections 12210-12213.

[5] Sec. 504. Rehabilitation Act of 1973, Pub. L. 93-112 (20 USC 794); sec. 11(a). Rehabilitation Act Amendment of 1974, Pub. L. 93-516, 88 Stat. 1619 (29 USC 706); sec. 606.

By 1978, Title IX compliance was mandated for postsecondary schools. Title IX's impact on educational programs in general is overshadowed by its impact on the educational programs of physical education, sports, and athletics. There are three required elements necessary to trigger Title IX's jurisdiction, and they are:

- gender discrimination,
- educational program, and
- federal funds.

Title IX does not prohibit race discrimination. It does not prohibit gender discrimination in noneducational programs, such as most private businesses. Neither does it prohibit gender discrimination in schools or other educational programs that receive no federal funds. So unless all three elements are present, Title IX doesn't apply. The elements needed to trigger Title IX jurisdiction are *not* the same as the Equal Protection clause of the 14th Amendment. For instance, Title IX applies whether or not a "state actor" is involved.

The law is found in one sentence. It is expanded on in the Regulations approved by Congress,[6] which have the force of law. Title IX's requirements, as they apply to athletics specifically, are found in the Policy Interpretations,[7] which do not have the force of law but which provide significant clout in delineating the law's requirements within sport programs. Together, the law, the Regulations, and the Policy Interpretations provide a reasonably clear picture concerning what would, in the context of physical education/sport/athletics constitute compliance with Title IX.

Today Title IX's jurisdiction is fully in force in all of the nation's elementary schools, junior high schools, high schools, and colleges that receive federal funding in any form. But its jurisdiction was not always full.

For the four-year period from 1984 to 1988, Title IX's jurisdiction over college-level athletics and physical education was removed. The removal of jurisdiction happened as a by-product of the U.S. Supreme Court's decision in *Grove City v. Bell*,[8] wherein the Court decided that although the indirect federal funding found at Grove City College was sufficient to trigger Title IX jurisdiction, once triggered, that jurisdiction applied only to the subunit of the institution

---

[6] *Federal Register*, Vol. 45, No. 92, May 9, 1980.

[7] *Federal Register*, Vol. 44, No. 239, December 11, 1979.

[8] 104 S. Ct. 1211 (1984).

that actually received the federal dollars. College physical education departments and athletics programs do not generally receive even indirect federal dollars, and so they were not within the jurisdiction of Title IX.

From the 1984 *Grove City* decision to the 1988 passage, over presidential veto, of the Civil Rights Restoration Act of 1987, athletics and physical education programs within the nation's colleges were not barred from gender discrimination by the provisions of Title IX. From 1984 to 1988, a student could walk across campus from the Biology Department (recipient of federal grants), where gender discrimination was prohibited by Title IX, to the Athletics Department, where the protections of Title IX did not exist.

The result of the *Grove City* decision seemed incongruous, but it remained in force until 1988, when Congress passed the Civil Rights Restoration Act, which (among other things), effectively restated the intent of Congress to have Title IX apply on an institution-wide basis rather than a subunit basis. Since 1988, it has been settled law that the entire institution is subject to the provisions of Title IX as long as the three elements are present.

Thirteen program components of athletics form the focus of any review of Title IX compliance. They are:

- athletic financial assistance,
- accommodation of interests and abilities,
- equipment and supplies,
- scheduling of games and practice times,
- travel and per diem allowance,
- tutors,
- coaches,
- locker rooms and practice and competitive facilities,
- medical and training facilities and services,
- housing and dining facilities and services,
- publicity,
- support services, and
- recruitment of student athletes.

The 13 program areas for athletics are found in the Policy Guidelines, and details of Title IX's requirements in physical education programs are found mainly in the Regulations.[9] But let's look at the athletics program areas briefly because they will give us an idea of how Title IX is supposed to work generally.

Benefit vs. dollars

The only place where the amount of dollars spent is of paramount significance in determining compliance is in the athletic financial assistance area. Everywhere else, the issue of equal treatment is framed in terms of benefit rather than dollars. For instance, if the female teams have the benefit of an inexperienced, part-time coach and the male teams have the benefit of highly experienced, full-time coaches, the institution would be out of compliance in the area of opportunity to receive coaching. It would not matter if the total dollars spent on coaches for male teams and female teams were the same either in the aggregate or per capita. What matters is benefit.

Dollars are the issue in the program component of athletic financial assistance. The law is quite clear and has withstood numerous challenges. The total number of financial aid dollars spent on the men's program, must be in proportion with the percentage of male participants in the athletic program, and the same formula is true for the females. Nationally, only about 30 to 40 percent of NCAA athletes are female. So let's look at the "average" school, Average University. If AU spends $100,000 on athletic financial aid and 35 percent of its athletes are females, it would, at least on this issue as currently interpreted, be in compliance if it spent $35,000 as athletic financial assistance for its female athletes. It is extremely important to add, however, that if AU's student body ratio is not also 35 to 65 percent, AU may be out of compliance in another significant area: accommodation of interests and abilities of the underrepresented sex.

Participation opportunities

Accommodation of interests and abilities of the underrepresented sex is a requirement of Title IX that has been taken seriously by the courts. A school has only three ways by which it can meet this requirement. The requirement will be met if:

---

[9] More information is available in *NAGWS Title IX Toolbox* (available from the National Association for Girls and Women in Sports, AAHPERD, 1900 Association Dr., Reston, VA 20191).

- the intercollegiate or interscholastic level of participation opportunities for male and female students is provided in numbers substantially proportionate to their respective enrollments, or
- the institution can show a history and continuing practice of program expansion that is demonstrably responsive to the developing interests and abilities of the underrepresented sex (almost always females in this context), or
- the institution can show that the interests and abilities of the members of that sex have been fully and effectively accommodated by the present program.

Few institutions have athletics programs that represent the gender make-up of their student bodies. Few institutions can show a sufficiently strong historical expansion.

Thus the only remaining way for an institution whose proportion of males and females in their athletics program doesn't substantially mirror their student body is for the female students to have no interest or ability. An athletics program that elects to offer a particular new team for women, and finds few women turn out for the team, may believe that no one is interested. However, this is not what is required by the law. The law requires a more affirmative and complete showing of no interest. If a "team's worth" of females are interested in forming a varsity team for which they are appropriately skilled (and the college is out of balance in its gender ratio), the college needs to find a way to create that team (assuming there is competition, and so on available within the geographic range that teams in the men's programs travel). This result is challenging to administrators who have tight budgets, but it is the law. Creative administrators will find creative solutions to such problems rather than risk outside enforcement.

Enforcement of Title IX

Three mechanisms are available for Title IX enforcement. They are:

- in-house complaint,
- Office for Civil Rights complaint, and
- lawsuit.

The person making the complaint or filing the lawsuit does not need to use one enforcement strategy before embarking on another.

The choice is purely that of the complainant.

In-house complaints. Such complaints can be made by anyone regardless of the presence or absence of an affiliation with the program or school. In-house complaints must be investigated by the institution's Title IX officer. Title IX requires that each institution have a designated Title IX officer, and the absence of such a person on campus is also a violation of Title IX, albeit easily remedied. Few complainants have found in-house complaints useful. Perhaps this is so because the Title IX officer is usually someone who is employed at the pleasure of the college's CEO and might be risking discontinued employment if significant violations were found.

Office for Civil Rights complaints. The OCR is charged with the administrative enforcement of Title IX initially; then, if OCR deems it appropriate, it will turn over a case to the Department of Justice for legal action. Anyone with or without "legal standing" (legal standing means the person has a stake in the outcome) may file an OCR complaint. Historically, OCR complaints have taken a long time to reach conclusion and have not always been as effective in increasing equity as victims might wish.

Lawsuits. Until February 1992, Title IX lawsuits were not the favored method of enforcement. They were expensive and when successful, yielded no monetary damages. In addition, only people with legal standing could file suit, thus generally limiting (in sports settings) the list of possible plaintiffs to participants, potential participants, and coaches. However, on February 26, 1992, the U.S. Supreme Court unanimously ruled in *Franklin v Gwinnett County Public Schools*[10]. The *Franklin* decision tells us that plaintiffs may sue for compensatory and punitive damages in cases alleging intentional discrimination under Title IX. The decision also indicates that the issue of intent would be easily overcome because of the law's requirement to have a Title IX officer in place. Thus it would be hard for an athletics program to actually discriminate without doing so intentionally. The Court seems to have reasoned that Title IX was 20 years old in 1992 when *Franklin* was decided and each campus was required to have a Title IX officer; therefore, if discrimination was still evident, it must have been intentional. Each passing year makes the court's logic even stronger. The availability of compensatory and punitive damages has changed enforcement strategies enormously.

---

[10] 112 S. Ct. 1028, 1992.

An administrator who wishes to fight Title IX allegations is no longer strategically correct to try to delay compliance.

The requirements of Title IX are of great importance in any program under its jurisdiction. We have only discussed a few of its requirements, but the process for the other areas is similar.

Title IX applies to all parts of the educational endeavor, not just athletics. Its application to junior and senior high school physical education has been a pedagogical challenge because it requires physical education classes to be taught on a coed basis. There are exceptions, such as courses involving contact sports, but generally coed classes are the rule.

Memory Testers—Title IX

1. True/False. Title IX requires a school to cut teams for males if the school's female teams are underfunded.
2. True/False. Title IX uses a quota system to force schools to increase the participation ratio of female athletes.
3. True/False. In most schools, males are not protected by Title IX.
4. True/False. Money and equipment coming into an athletics program from donations or booster clubs and reserved for a particular team does not count into the Title IX evaluation process.
5. True/False. Football and other sports purported to be "revenue" sports are *not* excluded from the requirements of Title IX.
6. True/False. If a school has the same number of teams for its males and females, it automatically meets the need to provide equal opportunity to participate.
7. True/False. A college which grants financial aid to its athletes must provide funding in proportion to the number of males and females in the athletics program.
8. True/False. If the teams in the males' program typically have more full-time coaches than in the females' program, or more assistant coaches than in the females' program, it is likely that a Title IX violation exists.
9. True/False. An athletics program must spend equal money on both its male and female programs in order to comply with Title IX.

Memory Tester Discussion

1. False.   Good educational philosophy dictates that both males and females benefit from high quality athletics programs. To cut one gender's opportunities to benefit another is poor administrative policy. The Office for Civil Rights has made it clear that cutting teams is *not* required or even recommended as a solution to budgetary or gender equity problems.

2. False.   A school has three ways to demonstrate that it has met the requirement to provide equal opportunity to participate for both sexes in its athletics program. The school can show a historic pattern and practice of upgrading its program for females (the historically underrepresented sex in most schools), or it can show that there are not unmet needs for participation among its females, or it can show that the ratio of athletes mirrors the ratio of males and females in the student body. Therefore, by definition, if there are no females with the interest in and ability to play, there is no need to drag them into the program to meet a nonexistent quota. The *Cohen v. Brown University* case made this point clearly.

3. True.   In athletics, females are typically the historically underrepresented sex. Title IX, unlike the 14th Amendment, protects only the historically underrepresented sex rather preventing gratuitous classification of **any** protected class. So in most circumstances, if a "minor" sport team for males is underfunded by its athletics administration, that team cannot look for help from Title IX, simply because the males on campus are not the historically underrepresented sex.

4. False.   It does not matter what the source of the money or equipment is. It does not matter if the donations are earmarked for a particular team. The athletic administration is required to provide equal benefit to its men's and women's programs. Therefore, if one

[11] 809 F. Supp 978, D.R.I. 1992, aff'd 991 F 2d 888 1993, 1996 U.S. App. Lexis 30192.

program receives benefits in the form of donations of equipment or funding, the athletic administration must find ways to provide equal benefits to the other gender's program.

5. True. The inclusion of football and other so-called, "revenue" sports within the jurisdiction of Title IX has been well-settled since the mid-1970s. The vast majority of such programs actually lose money, but even if they were truly revenue-producing sports, they are such, in large measure, because of the history of support they have received over the years at the expense of other men's and women's teams. To exclude them from Title IX would be sanctioning the creation and continuation of an underclass of sports struggling in a discriminatory setting.

6. False. It is not the number of teams but the number of participation slots (individual athletes) which is the basis for compliance determination. This is logical because some teams carry large rosters and others carry small rosters.

7. True. Financial aid is the only place where dollars spent rather than benefit provided is the measure of compliance.

8. True. The sex of the coaches is not a consideration under Title IX unless there is discrimination in the hiring or retention of the coach based on sex. However, the student athletes have a right under Title IX to have equal access to coaching. Therefore, if one gender only has part-time coaches or no assistant coaches and the other gender enjoys the benefits of full-time coaches and assistant coaches, there is a Title IX issue.

9. False. Other than financial aid (which must be provided with equal dollars based on proportion of athletics in the program), the school needs to provide equal benefit, not equal money.

Title VII

Title VII provides protection from discrimination on a variety of bases in the workplace. In part, Title VII says, "It shall be an unlawful employment practice for an employer . . . to discriminate against any individual with respect to . . . compensation, terms, conditions, or privileges of employment because of a person's: race, color, religion, national origin, or sex."

Title VII does not protect students; it only protects employees. Title VII is enforced by the EEOC (Equal Employment Opportunities Commission). The EEOC can investigate and conciliate, or sue on behalf of the plaintiff, or give the plaintiff permission to sue on his or her behalf. The EEOC can also create guidelines for enforcement and has done so in an area of interest to sports professionals: coaches' pay.[12] It has been quite useful in recent years in combating discrimination of teachers and coaches in areas related to pay as well as to working conditions in general. Title VII applies to any workplace which has 15 or more employees working 20 hours or more calender weeks and which has an impact on interstate commerce. The requirement of having an impact on interstate commerce is easily met.

Title VII's theories of liability fall into four main categories:

* systemic disparate treatment
  -employer's policies or the application of policies results in treatment which disfavors one group versus another
* Individual disparate treatment
  -employer's policies or the application of policies results in treatment which disfavors a particular individual based on that individual's membership in a protected class such as race, religion, sex, and so on who was an applicant for a job

  - applied for a job opening,
  - was qualified for the job,
  - was not hired, and
  - the position was filled with a non-class member or the position was left open.

---

[12] EEOC's *Guidance on Application of Anti-Discrimination Laws to Coaches' Pay at Education Institutions*, issued on October 31, 1997, is available via the internet at www.eeoc.gov/press/10-31-97.html or by writing EEOC's Office of Communications and Legislative Affairs, 1801 L Street, N.W., Washington, DC 20507.

- or who was an employee

    - who was performing satisfactorily

    - who was discharged or adversely affected by a change in working conditions

    - whose work was assigned to a nonprotected class member

- Disparate impact
  -an employer's policies are neutral, but their application produces a result which disfavors a particular individual or group
- Retaliation
  -an employer disfavors an individual who has exercised rights under anti-discrimination legislation

There are several affirmative (must be actively argued and proven by the defense) defenses within Title VII to allegations of discrimination. These are:

- seniority system,
- merit system,
- quantity and quality of production, and
- pay differential which is based on something other than membership in a protected class.

The fourth affirmative defense noted above (pay differential based on something other than membership in a protected class) might be used by proving that employee's pay is based on that employee's prior salary, or superior experience, education, and ability, or that the employee has more duties. These affirmative defenses must be proven, not merely alleged. The courts are becoming more sensitive to the fact that some defendants are using these defensesonly as pretext, and thus has actually engagd in discriminatory practices.

Equal Pay Act

The jurisdiction of the Equal Pay Act (EPA) is comparable to that of Title VII and it is enforced both by the courts and by the EEOC. The Equal Pay Act, unlike Title VII, applies only to sex discrimination. When using the EPA to claim discrimination, a comparator employee must be identified. That means that a comparable employee, carrying out comparable duties, must be identified by the plaintiff as a basis for comparing salaries. If there is no such employee within the workplace, EPA is not able to be used. Unlike the EPA, Title VII does not require that an comparison employee be identified. Rather, Title VII only requires a claim of discriminatory treatment or a showing of discriminatory impact in order to be a useful tool against discrimination in the workplace.

Section 504

Now that we've looked at the general pattern of statutory imperatives for equity via a brief review of Title IX, Title VII, and the Equal Pay Act, let's take a look at the area of disability legislation. Two major statutes relating to discrimination against people with disabilities are Section 504 of the Rehabilitation Act of 1973 (Section 504) and the Americans with Disabilities Act (ADA).

In the year following the passage of Title IX, Section 504 of the Rehabilitation Act of 1973 became law. Its language closely tracked the language of Title IX: "No qualified handicapped person shall, on the basis of handicap, be excluded from participation in, be denied the benefits of, or otherwise be subjected to discrimination under any program or activity that receives or benefits from federal financial assistance."

Take a moment to review the language of Title IX (above) and compare it with the Section 504 language. (Overlook the fact that Section 504 uses the older term "handicap" instead of "disability.") The elements required to trigger jurisdiction for Title IX and Section 504 are somewhat similar:

Title IX	Section 504
• gender discrimination	• handicap discrimination
• educational program	- - - - - -
• federal funds	• federal funds
- - - - - -	• qualified individual

Unlike Title IX, Section 504 does not contain a requirement that the discriminator be an educational program. There is, however, one additional hurdle that must be overcome in order to trigger jurisdiction of Section 504. With reasonable accommodation, the victim of the discrimination needs to be qualified. For instance, the employee-victim would need to be qualified to do the job (e.g., have computer skills if demanded by the job) if reasonable accommodation were made for their disability (e.g., wheelchair accessible computer terminal). The student-victim would need to meet the other requirements for school attendance (e.g., school age, GPA) if reasonable accommodation were made such as a sign language interpreter.

The U.S. Supreme Court's Title IX decision in *Grove City v. Bell* had a devastating yet temporary effect on Title IX's applicability to physical education and athletics programs. Because of the similarity in language between Title IX and Section 504, the *Grove City* decision posed similar jurisdictional limitations on Section 504 enforcement.

The 1988 passage of the Civil Rights Restoration Act of 1987 repaired Section 504's effectiveness in the same way it repaired the effectiveness of Title IX and other similarly worded legislation. Thus, Section 504 now applies to all parts of an institution or program that have any portion or subunit benefiting from federal financial assistance. It would be difficult to conceive of a school in the public sector and most in the private sector that are not now under Section 504's jurisdiction.

Section 504 protects "qualified handicapped persons" from discrimination. What is meant by the term "qualified handicapped person?" The Regulations tell us that the term refers to "any person who (i) has a physical or mental impairment which substantially limits one or more major life activities, (ii) has a record of such an impairment, or (iii) is regarded as having such an impairment."[13] Major life activities include "caring for one's self, performing manual tasks, walking, seeing, hearing, speaking, breathing, learning, and working."

Americans with Disabilities Act

Because the ADA and Section 504 are similar, let's now add the newer ADA to our discussion. Eighteen years minus a week after Title IX became law, the Americans with Disabilities Act was signed into law on June 16, 1990. The ADA's jurisdiction is expanded beyond programs receiving federal funds to include most employers, public ac-

---

[13] Regulations, §104.3 (j) (i), *Federal Register*, Vol. 45, No. 92, May 9, 1980, p. 30937.

commodations, and public services, whether or not they receive federal funding. ADA's jurisdiction is therefore much broader than that of Section 504, but that breadth has little additional effect on schools, because schools were already with under the jurisdiction of Section 504.

The ADA defines "qualified individuals with disabilities" in much the same way as Section 504 and indeed, in most ways, except for the expanded jurisdiction, simply reinforces Section 504 in the school setting and more fully defines and delineates its requirements.

Both the ADA and Section 504 apply to the educational setting. Both apply to students as well as employees. Both require an institutionally designated officer. Both are enforced in much the same way, with the Department of Education's Office for Civil Rights carrying the main enforcement burden along with the Equal Employment Opportunity Commission.

Let's take a look at some effects of Section 504 and ADA through the use of "*What If's*":

- What if a student is an abuser of drugs? When the school disciplines the student for the abuse, can the student claim discrimination under Section 504 or the ADA?

  No. It is made clear that employees or students currently using illegal drugs may be disciplined without violating either Section 504 or the ADA.

- What if a teacher used to abuse drugs but has successfully undergone a rehabilitation program and is no longer on drugs? Can the teacher be fired when the teacher's past record of drug abuse becomes known?

  No. A person who abused drugs or alcohol in the past would be protected. However, the ADA and Section 504 do not protect someone who is currently a drug or alcohol abuser.

- What if a school, in response to Section 504, makes a full program or set of activities accessible to its disabled students even though not all pre-1977 buildings are accessible. Can the student force the school to do more?

  Yes. Section 504 requires all construction after June 3, 1977, to be accessible, but pre-1977 buildings do not need to be updated if a full program or set of activities is accessible. Even though the basic requirements of removing architectural barriers are similar between the ADA and Section 504, the ADA adds the requirement that regardless of when a facility was built, barriers must be removed if such removal is "readily achievable." So, if there are additional barriers in those older buildings whose removal is readily achievable, they must be removed. This is true even if the student, without their removal, would already have access to a full program but not access to the full facility.

- What if during a job interview for a new coach, one of the interviewers asked, "Do you have AIDS or does anyone you associate with have AIDS?" Is such a question legal in the context of Section 504 and the ADA?

No. Medical questions are not appropriate at the interview stage. After a job offer is made, the potential employer may make inquiries of the candidate that are directly related to the candidate's ability to perform the job requirements.

Would having AIDS directly relate to the performance of the job? Not usually. If the coach had AIDS and the potential employer could successfully make the argument that the disease would be a direct threat to the health and safety of the coach and those around the coach, the employer must still try to relieve or reduce that threat through reasonable accommodation. The only way an employer could discriminate against someone who had AIDS would be if the disease, even after reasonable accommodation such as changing duties to omit contact sports or requiring first aid be performed by someone else, was still a direct threat to the health and safety of the coach or those around the coach.

The second part of the question relates to the people with whom the candidate associates. The law is clear: Discrimination based on associating with someone with a disability is illegal. Thus we arrive at the question, Is AIDS a disability? The answer is yes. Therefore it is illegal to discriminate against someone based on their association with a person who has AIDS.

Physical Education Major Requirements for the Disabled Student

If a student cannot complete a particular course required for a degree in physical education because of a disability, can that student be barred from becoming a physical education major without violating Section 504 or the ADA? The answer is, maybe.

In addition to providing appropriate assistance in the form of interpreters, more time for tests, and so on, specific course requirements may, where appropriate, need to be altered. However, subsection 104.44 of Section 504 tells us that maintaining "requirements which are essential to the program of instruction being pursued . . . or to any directly related licensing requirement will not be regarded as discriminatory."

Section 504 specifically discusses physical education and athletics. It specifically prohibits discrimination based on disability in physical education and athletics in the same way as in other programs. If the person is qualified, with reasonable accommodation, to participate, it is a violation of Section 504 to bar that person.

It is important to note that Section 504 also prohibits counseling students with disabilities toward more restrictive careers than non disabled students with the same interests and abilities, with the solitary exception that the counselor is allowed to provide factual information about licensing and certification requirements that may pose barriers (Section 504 §104.7[b]).

It would be a mistake, for instance, to automatically bar a wheelchair-bound student from a major in physical education. Instead, two other avenues must be explored:

- *Are those activities or courses that pose barriers for the wheel chair-bound student essential?* The essential nature of the activities or courses needs to be evaluated, not from the stand point of whether they are required for graduation but rather whether they are essential experiences, knowledge, or skills without which one cannot be a physical educator. For in stance, is it really essential that a physical educator be able to perform a handstand, or is it only essential that a physical educator know how to describe, analyze, and teach a hand stand?
- *Can the wheelchair-bound student successfully complete the essential degree requirements if reasonable accommodations are made?*

These two avenues of consideration take a little creativity and individual evaluation, but they provide for a legally correct response to the requirements of Section 504 and the ADA.

Sexual Harassment

Title VII and Title IX both prohibit sexual harassment but do so slightly differently. Title VII has defined two types of harassment:

quid pro quo and hostile environment. Title IX only directly addresses *quid pro quo* harassment but has adopted effectively, through case law, the hostile environment definition as well.

Quid pro quo relates to an exchange of actions between two parties: ":If you want a good grade in this class without working, all you need to do is . . ." or "Your vita is a little weak in the publications area—I'm sure someone as sensual as you can find a way to help me overlook your lack of publications when I review your promotions file." *Quid pro quo* sexual harassment is often an overt extortion of sexual behavior from students or employees. Even though it's overt to the victim, it's often difficult to prove.[14]

Hostile environment sexual harassment is just as significant as *quid pro quo* to the victim, but is even more difficult to prove. Instead of an exchange of actions, it involves actions by one party which are sufficiently severe or pervasive to create a sexually objectionable environment.

The Supreme Court (*Oncale*) doesn't require civility, nor does it prohibit "genuine but innocuous differences in the ways men and women routinely interact, offhand comments, [or] isolated incidents." But uninvited and offensive touching, lewd remarks, or speaking of the victim's gender or sexual orientation in derogatory terms can individually or together be sufficiently severe and pervasive to be actionable as hostile environment sexual harassment.

The United States Supreme Court, through a series of important decisions handed down during its 1997–1998 and 1998–1999 terms, has provided a clarity previously absent from discussions about the law and sexual harassment in the educational context. The Court's sexual harassment decisions are straightforward and leave few significant issues unclarified. The decisions apply directly to educational contexts and are specific enough to remove many of the old debate topics.

Among the issues the Court's decisions have clarified are the following:

- Sexual harassment can involve people of the same sex. It only requires that the harassment be based on sexual issues.

---

[14] S.E.S.A.M.E. is an organization focusing on sexual abuse and harassment by educators or other school employees in the school setting. It provides many useful materials. Contact D. Covello at 77 Paterson Avenue, Hempstead, NY 11550, 516-489-6406.

- Sexual harassment claims under Title VII do not require that the employer was aware of the peer harassment going on. Title IX claims of peer harassment do, however, require that the official with authority to intervene actually knew of the situation and reacted to that knowledge with deliberate indifference, thereby failing to stop the harassment.

Memory Testers

1. True/False. Title IX cannot be used in cases of sexual harassment.

2. True/False. Affirmative action means that you must always hire a minority group member or a women, even if they are not qualified.

3. True/False. Lack of money to expand the women's program is a viable excuse to use if your athletics program is accused of Title IX violations.

4. True/False. "Revenue" sports are not under the jurisdiction of Title IX.

5. True/False. Offensive remarks about sexual preference are not considered sexual harassment under the law.

6. True/False. When a student, teacher, or coach believes he or she has been the victim of discrimination because of a disability, that person must first exhaust all possible methods of review and make a complaint on campus before he or she can file a lawsuit or formal complaint off campus with the EEOC.

7. True/False. The provision of sign language interpreters, audio tapes of lectures, longer test-taking periods, and course requirement substitution are all among the "reasonable accommodations" that would be required of a school if needed to meet the specific needs of a qualified student with a disability.

8. True/False. Because the ADA prohibits the potential employer from asking medical questions at the interview stage, the use of drug tests for student applicants and athletes is similarly prohibited.

9. True/False. Your intramural program does not discriminate against people with disabilities, but an outside frater-

nity or sorority renting gymnasium space from you does not attempt to accommodate the needs of qualified individuals with disabilities. You are in trouble.

Memory Tester Discussion

1. False.   Title IX specifically includes sexual harassment as an area of coverage. In fact, the 1992 Supreme Court case, *Franklin v. Gwinnett*, which assured the accessibility of compensatory and the potential for punitive damages under Title IX, was a sexual harassment case.

2. False.   Affirmative action allows the employer to determine what qualifications are required for a particular job. The qualifications can be set as high or low as the employer wants. Once the qualifications are established by the employer, it is assumed under the law that any applicant who meets those qualifications would be suitable. If it were not so, the employer would have set different qualifications. So once the pool of qualified candidates has been established by the employer's own set of standards, affirmative action enters the picture and gives added weight to the hiring of women and minority group members from within the pool of qualified candidates.

3. False.   Lack of money is sad. Lack of money is bad. But lack of money is not an excuse for not correcting Title IX violations.

4. False.   In the early 1970s, when the Title IX Regulations were being drafted, the issue of whether to include revenue sports was widely debated and was even the subject of the unsuccessful Tower amendment. It has been settled law since the mid-1970s that revenue sports are under the jurisdiction of Title IX.

Since we are talking about money, let's correct another frequently misunderstood area of Title IX. That area relates to the sources of funding within an athletic program. It is erroneous to believe that gifts to teams generated by alumni contacts, bake sales, car washes, and so on are not counted into the Title IX "piggy bank." If, for instance, someone donates 20 pairs of shoes for the men's team, the same level of benefit (new shoes at the same level of quality and quantity) needs to be provided for the women from whatever funding source exists. Source of funding is irrelevant.

5. False.

Sexual harassment falls into several categories. One category is *quid pro quo* harassment. *Quid pro quo* harassment exists when someone is induced into giving or accepting sexual favors, harassment, etc. in exchange for a better grade, relief from a term paper, and so on. The other category is called the hostile environment form of sexual harassment. The remarks in our questions would probably fall into this second category. Remarks that have a nexus to sexuality, sexual activity, or other sex related topics, if they create a sufficiently hostile (uncomfortable) environment, constitute sexual harassment.

Sexual harassment can be the subject of a number of statutory imperatives such as Title IX and Title VII, plus the 14th Amendment. The 1984 Policy Statement on Sexual Harassment issued by the Equal Employment Opportunity Commission (charged with the enforcement of Title VII cases) contains a statement defining some of the facets of sexual harassment in the workplace:

"a. Unwelcome sexual advances, requests for sexual favors, and other verbal or physical conduct of a sexual nature constitute sexual harassment when

(1) submission to such conduct is made either explicitly or implicitly a term or condition of an individual's employment,

(2) submission to or rejection of such conduct by an individual is used as a basis for employment decisions affecting such individual, or

(3) such conduct has the purpose or effect of unreasonably interfering with an individual's work performance or creating intimidating, hostile, or offensive working environment."

The guidelines refer to workplace harassment, but the law has evolved to make similar definitions applicable to student and athlete situations as well.

6. False.   Unlike some union grievance procedures, there is no requirement that a complainant initially or ever use the in-house complaint procedure for ADA or Section 504 violations. Both the ADA and Section 504 require that in-house complaint procedures be in place, but their use is not required. The complainant can make the initial complaint to the appropriate governmental agency without ever having said a word to anyone on campus. Such a decision to go off campus may not be the best if people of good will exist on campus ready to make appropriate accommodations, but the complainant remains free to select the starting point for the complaint process.

7. True.   The ADA and Section 504's views of reasonable accommodation include a variety of items that have budgetary impact. Those in charge of enforcement are unmoved by the excuse that a program's budget has not included sufficient funds to provide for an accommodation deemed to be reasonable for a disabled student or employee. About 10 percent of students and staff on campus have some sort of disability that falls within the jurisdiction of Section 504 or the ADA. Thus the prudent administrator builds into the budget appropriate funds to meet the needs for reasonable accommodation under Section 504 and the ADA.

8. False.   The ADA and Section 504 neither support nor bar the use of drug testing for student athletes.

9. True.   When you provide significant assistance, such as renting space to a fraternity or sorority, you have an affirmative duty to assure yourself that the outside organization's practices do not permit discrimination barred by Section 504 or the ADA. Affirmative duty means that you must seek out information, not just wait for it to arrive.

A Note About Federal Anti-Discrimination Legislation

Several cases involving Congress' Article 3 powers and the 11th Amendment have found their way to the U.S. Supreme Court. The issues involved relate to whether Congressional legislation can abrogate the states' sovereign immunity. What does this have to do with Title IX and Title VII and their friends? It is possible that the pending decisions of the Supreme Court in the 11th Amendment cases may make it impossible to sue a state based on federal legislation such as anti-discrimination laws. To be able to sue, the particular legislation involved would have to be shown to have been enacted to enforce the due process clause of the 14th Amendment as well as other items. The issues are complex and convoluted; the potential impact is great however. Just keep your eyes on the news so you'll be the first one on your block to understand whatever the Supreme Court decides on the issue of sovereign immunity of the states in relation to federal legislation.

Risk Management and the Equity Issues

The prudent administrator realizes that in addition to the legal imperatives for conducting equitable programs, there exist, more than in most other areas of the law, educational and moral imperatives also. The prudent administrator also realizes that, from a risk management standpoint, it is necessary to be aware of the requirements of at least the following legal imperatives for equity enforcement:

- Title IX of the Education Amendments of 1972—protects students and employees from sex discrimination.
- Equal Pay Act, 1963—protects employees from sex discrimination in pay.
- Title VI, Civil Rights Act of 1964—protects students from discrimination based on race and national origin.
- Title VII, Civil Rights Act of 1964- protects employees from discrimination on the basis of race, sex, national origin, and religion.
- Executive Order 11246 as amended by Executive Order 11375, 1968—protects employees against discrimination on the basis of race, sex, national origin, and religion.

- Rehabilitation Act, 1973 Section 504 (29 U.S.C.A. 3794) (integrated into the Civil Rights Restoration Act of 1987—pro tects employees and students from discrimination on the ba sis of handicaps.
- Education for All Handicapped Children Act, Public Law 94-142, 1976 (20 U.S.C.A. §1401 et seq.—protects students from discrimination on the basis of handicaps.
- Pregnancy Discrimination Act, 1978—protects employees from discrimination based on sex (pregnancy).
- Age Discrimination in Employment Act, amended 1978- protects employees from age discrimination.
- Americans with Disabilities Act, 1992—protects a wide range of individuals against discrimination based on handicapping conditions.

Hold harmless laws do not cover discriminatory acts. Insurance, if it addresses discriminatory acts at all, only covers the defense costs of a defendant who is ultimately found not guilty. Thus the best risk management techniques involve avoiding problems to begin with—always good advice. The following suggestions may apply with more or less specificity to the various anti-discrimination laws, but all are useful to some degree:

- Develop, adopt and promulgate policies.
- Conduct training programs for all.
- Practice what you preach.
- Develop risk-free reporting mechanisms.
- Respond to all complaints promptly and consistently.
- Hire good supervisors.
- Monitor complaints.
- Have a zero tolerance for sexual harassment.
- Do not retaliate.
- Define sexual harassment and give examples.
- Provide clear grievance procedures, including alternative routes for complaints.
- Make it clear where to report.
- Maintain confidentiality for all concerned in sexual harassment complaints.
- Identify possible disciplinary actions for sexual harassment perpetrators.

- Work with state and federal enforcement agencies and seek their input.
- Spell out required actions for observers of harassment and other violations.
- Decide on policy for consensual amorous relationships.
- Define appeals process.

How About Looking Up a Few Cases and Guidelines?

If you're near a law library, you might find it interesting to read some of the following cases. Some have value as precedents within their jurisdictions, others don't. Don't assume that the outcome would be the outcome in your jurisdiction. Read them to gain an insight into how the issues of equity and equality are evaluated. As you read them, develop arguments of your own for the plaintiff and then for the defendant.

Cohen v. Brown University, 809 F. Supp. 978, (D.R.I.(1992) (Cohen, aff'd 991 F 2d 888 (1st Cir. 1993) (Cohen II). This Title IX case reaffirms the methods of meeting the interests and abilities component of the Policy interpretations.

Davis v. Monroe County Board of Education. (97-843). U.S. Supreme Court, (1999). This case involves sexual harassment of an elementary school student by a classmate. The school failed to act effectively to stop the harassment. The issue is "notice."

Faragher v. City of Boca Raton (970282). Decided by the Supreme Court on June 26, 1998. This case discusses the employer's liability for harassment by a supervisor of a lifeguard employee.

Favia v. Indiana University of Pennsylvania, 812 F. Supp. 578, motion to modify order denied, 7 F. 3d 332 (3d Cir. 1993). This Title IX case involved court-ordered reinstatement of teams.

Franklin v. Gwinnett, County Public Schools, 112 S. Ct. 1028 (1992). This landmark Supreme Court case has changed the enforcement strategies for Title IX because of its decision concerning compensatory and punitive damages.

Gebser v. Lago Vista Independent School District (96-1866). Decided by the Supreme Court on June 22, 1998. This case discusses the need of notice of the employer in harassment between a student and teacher.

Grove City College v. Bell, 465 U.S. 555 (1984). This is the Title IX case that removed jurisdiction from college-level athletic and physical education programs from 1984 to 1988.

NCAA v. Smith. No. 98-84, Supreme Court of the United States, 525 U.S. 84; 119 S. Ct. 924; 142 L. Ed. 2d 929 (1999). This case deals with whether the NCAA's receipt of dues triggers Title IX jurisdiction.

Oncale v. Sundowner Offshore Services. 523 U.S. 1998. This case deals with same-sex sexual harassment.

School Board of Nassau County v. Arline, 480 U.S. 273, 107 S. Ct. 1123 (1987). This Supreme Court case focuses on the definition of "handicapped individual" as it is defined by the Rehabilitation Act of 1973.

Wright v. Columbia University, 520 F. Supp. 789 (1981). Should an athlete with a vision defect be allowed to participate in football and risk losing vision?

Chapter 14
Defusing Liability:
Managing the Risks

In earlier chapters we have discussed specific risk management techniques for various causes of action. The overriding principle for all risk management techniques is to identify, evaluate, and then determine how to manage risks.

In the area of negligence, there are many techniques available to manage risk through transferring it to others, such as by insurance, waivers, and so forth. (See Chapter 6 for a full discussion of these techniques.) In other areas of the law, risk management techniques fall more in the area of prevention. (See specific chapters relating to specific areas of the law for risk management discussions.) But in order to prevent, you must still be able to identify.

Proper procedures, frequent review of programmatic activities and policies, and an awareness of legal issues relating to risk management are all helpful in the process.

Develop Proper, Prudent Procedures

Developing and following prudent procedures can do much to manage risks. Thinking about creating and practicing medical emergency plans and keeping records appropriately, and using proper interview questions when hiring new staff are only two examples of managing risks.

Since we haven't talked about it much before, let's talk for a moment about proper interview questions. It is a good idea for the interviewers to agree on the questions ahead of time so that all interviewees are asked the same questions. Questions need to be job performance oriented. So if you want to know if a job applicant will be available for Saturday and Sunday work, don't ask if he or she is religious (thus assuming that the applicant's religious activities will get in the way of their working weekends). Instead, ask, "Is there any reason why you couldn't be scheduled for weekend work?" The first question is inappropriate because it is none of your business if the applicant is religious. It is also a potential violation of Title VII.

Another example of an inappropriate interview question would be, "Do you have family or children in school?" Probably what you are trying to find out is, "Will there be any difficulties with having to relocate your residence if you take this job?" and that is exactly what you should be asking rather than inquiring about the applicant's marital or family status.

Prudent procedures include developing and using accident/incident reports. Accident or incident reports help memorialize the facts of situations that might later produce legal action. Accident or incident reports should be carefully drafted to memorialize the facts but not to assign fault. Assignment of fault will occur when litigation develops. It is foolish to create judgments of fault that may be erroneous in a legal sense through accident or incident reports instead of letting the judicial process assign fault. Why volunteer for liability that might not actually be yours to accept? So, don't include questions on the accident or incident report such as, "Was there any failure with the equipment?" or "Was there any defect in the facilities which needed to be corrected?"

Understand Legal Time Periods

Statutes of limitation set time periods within which a plaintiff must begin a lawsuit. Records of incidents and accidents should be kept on file at least until the appropriate statute of limitation has run to conclusion. When an incident occurs that might produce liability, it is a wise administrator who stays in contact with witnesses over the years it often takes to arrive at either the litigation process or conclusion of the statute of limitations. Staff members or students who served as witnesses may have moved to other employment or schools and changed addresses by the time a case comes to trial, thus leaving the defendant who has not kept in touch without access to important witnesses.

The normal statutes of limitations that apply to adults are applied differently to minors. When a minor has been injured, the minor has until adulthood before the statute of limitations runs out. For instance, in most jurisdictions in which a child becomes an adult at 18, the statute of limitations will be tolled (suspended for a period of time) until the plaintiff becomes 18 plus one year. Therefore, when working with young children, records of incidents and accidents may need to be kept for an extremely long period of time.

Memory Testers

1. True/False. It is illegal to breach a contract.
2. True/False. Insurance will protect me from damages resulting from intentional torts.
3. True/False. It is not more expensive to shift all risk to someone else through buying insurance.
4. True/False. The best risk-shifting plan is to plan to run high quality, safe programs.
5. True/False. Interview questions asked of a potential employee may include topics such as marital status, number of children, and religion.

Memory Tester Discussion

1. False.   It is *not* illegal to breach a contract. However, you might have to pay damages for the breach. If you think you might have to breach a contract, you should try to include language in the original contract which relieves you from your obligations under the contract. If that is not possible, then consider adding a liqui-

dated damages clause to the contract so that you will know the amount of damages you might be incurring ahead of time.

2. False.   Insurance is only designed to protect from ordinary negligence. It is contrary to public policy to let people shift the risk of liability from themselves to others for their intentional acts.

3. False.   Insurance coverage will be greater if the deductible is lower. Assuming some of the risk by agreeing to pay claims up to the amount of a deductible is cheaper.

4. True.   However, even the best programs sometimes make mistakes. A risk management plan is a proactive plan. It plans for the worst while hoping for the best and, indeed, planning for the best program.

5. False.   The marital status of a job applicant is irrelevant in most conceivable circumstances to the performance of a particular job. Therefore, it is a question the smart and astute interviewer would avoid. In addition, such questions as number of children or religion, even if innocently asked, are often actionable. If you want to know about an applicant's likelihood of having to be frequently absent from work because of family duties, the questions should be framed in a direct way. For instance, "Do you anticipate that any outside obligations will cause you to arrive late or be absent from work on a frequent basis?" That's really what you want to know—not whether someone is married or has children.

In Conclusion

Let's add two last points to remember:

- When managing risks, it is important to know that innocence is not free. Therefore, risk management plans need to include provisions for paying for the defense of claims.

- Legal liability comes to both programs and individuals. Risk management should be part of any program's activities. It should also be part of the activities of an individual teacher, coach, or administrator.

Appendix

There are many internet sites which provide easy access to the cases listed at the conclusion of many of this book's chapters. You'll find an asterisk next to a few of the more comprehensive sites. The "http://www." has been omitted for ease of reading the citations. All of the listings are free. The sites listed, plus, at times particular state court decisions you can link to, will provide all the starting navigational points you'll need.

These two sites are the most inclusive and complete.
- law.cornell.edu
- FindLaw.com

These three sites are very useful for federal issues.
- supct.law.cornell.edu (Supreme Court only)
- fedcir.gov
- eeoc.gov/press (source of Title VII and Equal Pay Act guidance)

1c.loc.gov/global/judiciary.htm1

law.emory.com

law.villanova.edu

ny1j.com

access.gpo.gov

Index